THE GREATEST ACHIEVEMENT IN LIFE

FIVE TRADITIONS OF MYSTICISM
– *and* –
MYSTICAL APPROACHES TO LIFE

THE GREATEST ACHIEVEMENT IN LIFE

FIVE TRADITIONS OF MYSTICISM
– and –
MYSTICAL APPROACHES TO LIFE

R.D. KRUMPOS

Palomar Print Design, Publisher
Tucson, Arizona

THE GREATEST ACHIEVEMENT IN LIFE
Five Traditions of Mysticism
Mystical Approaches to Life

Copyright © 2022
R. D. Krumpos

Published by Palomar Print Design.
All rights reserved.

No part of this book may be used or reproduced in any manner whatsoever without written permission except in the case of brief quotations embodied in critical articles and reviews.

For information contact:
Palomar Print Design
Tucson, Arizona
www.palomarprint.com

Proofread by Dr. Paul C. Martin at The University of Adelaide.

Dedicated to Bridget Brown of Solarity Design
for her invaluable assistance.

Book design by Palomar Print Design

Cover Image: Orion Nebula, birthplace of the stars in our Galaxy.
Courtesy of NASA, ESA, M. Robberto
(Space Telescope Science Institute/ESA)
and the Hubble Space Telescope Orion Treasury Project Team

The greatest achievement in life: Five traditions of mysticism and Mystical approaches to life / R. D. Krumpos.

ISBN 978-0-578-39566-1

Contents

FIVE TRADITIONS OF MYSTICISM

1. Introduction 1
2. What's in a Word? 5
3. Mysticism Defined 9
4. What is Reality? 13
5. Prominent Mystics 17
6. Mystic Viewpoints 31
7. The Divine Is Not 39
8. Mysticism Is Not 43
9. To the Non-Religious 51
10. Warnings! 59
11. Reality Is One 67
12. Preconditions to Learning 75
13. Love, Knowledge and 83
14. Some Differences 87
15. Primary Bibliography 91

MYSTICAL APPROACHES TO LIFE

16. The Big Picture 105
17. Our Different Worlds 109
18. A Divine Formula? 117
19. Upside Down 121
20. Looking Beyond 125
21. Feel Good—Do Good 133
22. Discard, Abandon and Realize 137
23. Beyond Words 141
24. Oneness in Separateness 145
25. Finding the Soul 149
26. A Little of This, a Little of That 153
27. Heads Up! 157
28. The Grand Excuse 161
29. Contemporary Views 165
30. Beyond Me 169
31. Beyond Other 173
32. Wake Up! 177
33. Outside the Box 181

OTHER CONSIDERATIONS

34. Divine Laity 187

35. Duel of the Dual 191

36. Asleep 195

37. Be Realistic 199

38. Mystics' Consciousness 203

39. Specialized Bibliography 209

40. Secondary Bibliography 217

FIVE TRADITIONS OF MYSTICISM

Introduction

THE FIRST ESSAY, *What's in a Word?*, briefly outlines some of the fundamental differences between five of the largest religions and among the principal divisions in each faith. The following essays attempt to summarize many similarities among the mystical traditions in those religions. The 120 quotations of mystics highlight common views.

Essays are based on talking with mystics in twelve countries and 180 books ... 100 in the primary bibliography. Many people were consulted, including the directors of a Buddhist Center and of the Eastern Orthodox theological institute at two major universities, a Vedanta Society swami, the director of an Islamic Center, the director of a Reform theological college, the abbot of a Theravada temple, a Cistercian monk, a Hindu abbess, a Sufi shaikha, and a professor at a university for Judaism, plus ten professors who each teach courses on comparative mysticism. Their suggestions led to many revisions.

The practices and/or systems of these five traditions of mysticism do vary widely, employing dissimilar terminology and concepts. These essays use generally acceptable terms and note alternate words and definitions when appropriate. Some of the quotations from mystics (Buddhism, Christianity, Hinduism, Islam, and Judaism):

"One Nature, perfect and pervading, circulates in all natures. One Reality, all-comprehensive, contains within itself all realities." Yung-chia Ta-shih (B)

> Note: (685–713) Disciple of Hui-neng

"To gauge the soul we must gauge it with God, for the Ground of God and the Ground of the soul are one and the same." Meister Eckhart (C)

"Wherever you look … see that one unique Presence, indivisible and eternal, is manifested in all the universe. That is because God impregnates all things." Anandamayi Ma (H)

"Behold the One in all things; it is the second that leads you astray." Kabir (I/H)

"There exists nothing which is not united to Him and which He does not find in His own essence."
Moses Cordovero (J)

"One in all, all in One. If only this is realized, there is no worry about not being perfect."
The Third Patriarch of Zen [Seng ts'an] (B)

"Eternally, all creatures are God in God. So far as they are in God, they are the same life, same essence, same power, same One, and nothing less." Henry Suso (C)

"For the Self [soul] is not the ego; it is one with the All and the One and in finding it it is the All and the One that we discover in our Self." Sri Aurobindo (H)

"I went from God to God, until they cried from me, 'O thou I.'" Bayazid of Bistun (I)

"They are then actually united with the Divine Essence and, in all aspects, your soul is included with them."
Israel ben Eliezer [Ba'al Shem Tov] (J)

"The great path has no gates, thousands of roads enter it. When one passes through this gateless gate he walks freely between heaven and earth." Zen poem (B)

"The soul lives by that which it loves rather than in the body which it animates. For it has not its life in the body, but rather gives it to the body and lives in that which it loves." St. John of the Cross (C)

"Liberation cannot be achieved except by the perception of the identity of the individual spirit with the universal Spirit." Shankara [Sankara] (H)

"I am He whom I love, and He whom I love is I. We are two spirits in one body. If thou seest me, thou seest Him. And if thou seest Him, thou seest us both." Hallaj (I)

"A man should actually detach his ego from his body until he has passed through all the worlds and become one with God." Maggid of Mezerich [Dov Baer of Mezerich] (J)

True mystics had direct experience in divine union. Within these essays, *oneness, union* and *unity* all mean to be consciously in the unifying divine essence. These are some terms which are used in mysticism most often, but they are simply words. What *is* is not changed by what it is called. People's opinions too often distort it.

Note: Comparative religions use BCE or CE, Common Era, for the Christian BC or AD; ca. is approximate. The religious calendar varies among each of the five faiths.

What's in a Word?

THE WORD GOD, as used in English, is *Allah* in Arabic, *Brahman* in Sanskrit and *ha-Shem* (the Name) in Hebrew. God is *Theos* in Greek, the first written language of the New Testament. *Nirvana* in Buddhist Sanskrit can also mean absolute Truth: ultimate Reality.

Hinduism had no one founder; the Vedas advanced orally about 200 years before being recorded in Sanskrit from ca. 1300–600 BCE. The Hebrew Bible developed at least 300 years after Moses, ca. 1000–400 BCE. Siddharta Gautama had been born a Hindu and taught in Prakrit; Buddhism's first written canon was in Pali nearly 400 years later, ca. 17 BCE. Jesus was born a Jew and preached in Aramaic; the New Testament had evolved from ca. 100–367 CE. Muhammad spoke Arabic; the written Qur'an was formed within 30 years of his death in 632 CE. Scholars do not agree on those dates.[*]

Hindu scriptures also refer to *Ishvara*, a more personal aspect of Brahman, and often to *Vishnu* and *Shiva*, two of Brahman's triad, plus manifestations in Krishna and Rama. The Hebrew Bible uses the sacred, unspoken, *YHVH (YHWH)* for God; *Adonai* replaces it when reading

---

[*] Some scholars say that the oral traditions of Hindu and Jewish texts were first written in the 3rd Century BCE and the New Testament in the 1st Century CE (AD).

Jewish scriptures. Ha-Shem is used in conversation. Mahayana and Vajrayana vehicles may consider the *Dharmakaya* ("dharma-body" or Buddha-nature) more correct than Nirvana, final realization of the Theravada. In the first written New Testament, Jesus referred to God as *Abba* (Father) and Lord applied to both the persons of the Father and the Son in the Trinity. In the Qur'an, *al-Haqq* (the Truth, the Reality) is supremely the title of Allah. Islam has "99 Beautiful Names" for Allah's perfection; other faiths credit many attributes to God. In English, Absolute, Almighty, Creator, Diety and other words are used to refer to God; divine, holy, omnipotent, omniscient, and other adjectives usually apply only to God.

Many other religions have different words for God and a few, as in Buddhism, do not include a Supreme Being or Creator. Some give God personal qualities, while most speak of God as a spiritual omnipresence or an all-pervading force. Among the other religions which are still practiced today: Aboriginal traditions, African tribal beliefs, Baha'i, Druze, Jainism, Native American faiths, Polynesian spirit worship, Shinto, Sikhism, Taoism, Tenrikyo, Yoruba, and Zoroastrianism. Later prophets had developed new traditions, like Jewish Kabbalah, had gained new revelations, as in The Church of Jesus Christ of Latter-day Saints (Mormons), or had founded new religions, such as Baha'i. There are hundreds of religions and faiths.

The Vedas, most sacred to Hindus, were rejected by Buddhists who also defined many Sanskrit words differently, e.g. nirvana. The first five books of the Hebrew

Bible, the Torah, are most revered by Jews and are studied by most Christians. Practices and customs may vary between countries, as apparent among the predominately Muslim states, or blend in local mythology, such as in Hinduism on Bali. Doctrine for any one religion may differ between its divisions or their branches, like within the many Protestant denominations.

In Vedanta, Brahman is considered as the One God; Hindus of Shaivism, Shaktism and Vaishnavism may worship a chosen god, goddess or incarnation who emanates from Brahman. In Judaism, behavior and worship may vary among movements: Conservative, Hasidic, Orthodox, and Reform. Mahayana Buddhists rely on guidance of others and prayer; Theravada stresses self-reliance and good works; Vajrayana has secret rituals and metaphysics. Eastern Orthodox, Protestant, Roman Catholic, and other Christians may differ on grace, the Trinity and sources of doctrine. Ibadi, Shi'a and Sunni Islamic sects disagree on Muhammad's successors and on the status of imams; Sufi orders among them may worship differently.

Hindu texts written in classical Sanskrit sometimes changed when translated into India's 22 modern languages or into English. The Hebrew Bible varied in Greek and Latin; except for Protestants, the canon of Christianity's Old Testament included many books not in Judaism's canon. Buddhist texts in Pali and Sanskrit were often interpreted differently in other Asian languages and Ch'an/Zen downplays the use of scriptures. The New Testament has had many changes during translations, literal and idiomatic. The Qur'an was written only in Arabic for more than 1,200 years; first translations were in the early 1900's, but are not considered true Qur'an.

Reading the mystics of all religions can help to overcome these many apparent differences. Mysticism's message seems to be a consensus: The essence of the One is the essence of All. Although the ultimate Reality is the same, each experience of it can vary. That applies to each mystic as well as between mystics.

> Note: The five major religions are mentioned in order of their usual historical origins. All had originated in Asia (India and the Near East), but Judaism, Christianity and Islam are herein referred to as "Western" (yet the largest Muslim populations are in Indonesia, Pakistan, Bangladesh, and India). Mysticism is a tradition in some other faiths, too. Shinto of Japan—arguably larger than Judaism—worships "kami," heavenly and earthly divine powers shared by some humans ... not as mystics.

Mysticism Defined

Oxford Dictionary of World Religions
Edited by John Bowker. Published by Oxford University Press 1997, 2005

Mysticism: "The practices and often systems of thought which arise from and conduce toward mystical experience. Mystical systems are distinguished from other metaphysical systems by their intimate connection to a quest for salvation, union and/or liberation realized through forms of mental, physical and spiritual exercise in a classic definition. Mysticism, according to its historical and psychological definitions, is the direct intuition or experience of God; a mystic is a person who has, to a greater or lesser degree, such a direct experience; one whose religion and life are central not merely on an accepted belief or practice, but on that which he regards as first-hand personal knowledge."

Note: Non-theistic religions, such as Buddhism, seek the same ultimate Reality, but it is not conceived as God.

Judaism: "Kabbalah is teachings of the Jewish mystics. The term encompasses all the esoteric teachings of Judaism which evolved from the time of the second Temple. More particularly, it refers to those forms which evolved in the Middle Ages. Kabbalah draws on the awareness of the transcendence of God, and yet of his immanence. God can most closely be perceived through contemplation and illumination. God both conceals and reveals himself. Through speculation and revelation, the hidden life of God and his relationship with his creation can be more easily understood. Since mystical knowledge can so easily be misinterpreted its spread should be limited to those of a certain age and level of learning."

Note: The Zohar emphasized contemplation; Kabbalah of Hasidism added enthusiasm.

Concise Guide to World Religions
Eliade, Couliano. Published by HarperCollins San Francisco 1991, 2000

Christianity: " ... a brief survey of the rich mystical tradition of Christianity, which can be envisaged as a form of Platonic contemplative asceticism integrated with devotional and often liturgical activities. In its multifarious historical occurrences, Christian mysticism embraces almost all available mystical phenomenology, emphasizing to almost the same extent both ecstasy and introspection. The mystical experience tends toward the union with God in the complete surrender of the body and the world."

Note: Eastern Orthodox mysticism seeks union with the Godhead through the three persons, followed by a "deified" participation in life. All Friends (Quakers) should seek the Inner Light, follow divine leadings and regard all of life as sacramental.

MYSTICISM DEFINED

World Religions-Ancient History to Present
Geoffrey Parrinder. Published by Facts on File 1971, 1985

Islam: "The objective of Sufism, as all mysticism, is to attain union with God. Mysticism seeks for an immediate experience of the divine reality through the suppression of the ego. The method of attaining this most coveted experience, however, demands insight into a special and hidden brand of knowledge. Sufi doctrine teaches that, beside the usual rules for religious life, set out in the revelation and the prophetic sunnah, there is another and deeper level of spiritual meaning, which the prophet shared with only a few of his chosen companions. The revelation, thus, wears two faces, one open and obvious, and the other only to be seen by those who have been instructed in its secrets."

New Penguin Handbook of Living Religions
John R. Hinnells. Published by Penguin 1997, 2003

Hinduism: "Another concept, central and essential to Hinduism, is moksha (liberation), which is also one of the four Hindu aims of life. That from which liberation is sought is samsara, the cycle of birth and rebirth. The part of the human individual which is immortal ... passes at death to diverse heavens and hells where it works out its karmic debt and is then reborn in the form it has deserved. This cycle continues endlessly unless it merits, or is blessed with, a lifetime during which, through spiritual efforts, the intervention of a guru or the grace of God, moksha is attained, whereby it passes out of the cycle altogether."

Note: The notion of interim heavens and hells is not supported by all Hindu schools.

Buddhism: "The main aim is to emphasize immediate accessibility of direct realization. Enlightenment is to be striven for and realized in this very life. Ch'an [Zen] teachers claimed a transmission outside doctrines—direct and wordless communication between teacher and pupil. Later tradition lays great stress on this transmission. Practical action was to be preferred to study. Ch'an [Zen] often stresses the suddenness of realization of enlightenment, but in fact different degrees of realization were usually recognized."

Note: All Buddhism seeks enlightenment; Ch'an/Zen and Tibetan Tantrism may be regarded as more "mystical." The term "mysticism" is seldom used by Buddhists.

What is Reality?

TRUTH IS ONE, although people call it by many names. The world's religions honor prophets, messengers and/or incarnations: Krishna, Moses, Buddha, Jesus, Muhammad, and others throughout the ages. They have all sought to bring people closer to the divine. In the mystical tradition of religions, we can directly experience the divine in this life by giving up our ego and individuality to be in the soul, then consciously sharing in the unitive divine essence.

Spiritual liberation is the final objective, yet it must be sought in stages. Our attachment to our outer self, and its interaction with the external world, blinds us to the serenity of experiencing our inner self flowing within the universal whole. Few people are aware that the divine essence is the essence of All. *That art Thou*, the divine is in you, is a declaration of many scriptures; most mystics believe that essence to be the ultimate, eternal Reality. It is here and now.

Our inner self, or soul, is far more real than our ego self, which is cloaked in various names, shapes and circumstances. Someone's full name, their outward description and occupation tell very little about the true nature of the person. Also, many people often use external means to contemplate the divine: sacred scriptures, houses of worship, shrines, or sacred art forms. They can provide a light to guide us away from mundane concerns for survival, satisfaction and success, still none of them can entirely convey the spiritual Reality of the divine. Physical and mental appearances can be restricting.

It is not easy to leave the countless attractions of the material world nor the myriad of thoughts in the mind. Most religions use chanting, singing, dancing, recitation, and/or prayer to help us put aside our worldly activities to temporarily focus on the divine. Simple meditation can bring us centering inner peace. Our ego self then returns us to the limited realities perceived by our senses and minds to interact with our physical and social environment.

How can we realize enlightenment, or complete intuitive insight into unity with the divine, in one lifetime when the modern human race has not achieved perfection in 40,000 years (400,000 for homo sapiens)? Many people believe in only a single life, which might qualify us for an eternal afterlife. Others think we must live through numerous lives until we are in conscious oneness with the divine.

Why were we each born with our individual attributes, family and place? Those who believe in rebirth understand that our circumstances at birth result from our conduct in a past life. Many persons call seeming good fortune and bad luck *divine will*. Others name it *divine justice*, the consequences or reactions caused by our own actions in this or previous lives. Some scientists say it is chance or genetic.

Many mystics view this life as theater. Following *divine law* we must perform according to our script, but only to please the divine, the producer and director, not for the applause of the audience or the praise of fellow actors. People usually act to achieve personal benefits and believe that their characters and the play are reality. Our ultimate goal is to be aware of universal Reality as the true stage of life, released from attachment to our fictitious human roles.

Any religion in practice was affected by the circumstances of history and its rules and rituals are an interpretation by its leaders of what its believers must do to follow divine teachings. What might seem necessary for today, or for one person, may not be correct for tomorrow or for another person. We must seek our own liberation from mundane reality; for mystics this means to gain freedom from our limited self to realize oneness with the limitless divine.

Mysticism seeks to join, or unite, our inner self with the divine by spiritual disciplines of devotion, knowledge, selfless service, and/or meditation. What you do matters greatly to what you will become: that is divine justice. How you do it, through Islam, Christianity, Buddhism, Judaism, Hinduism, or outside these faiths is important when it is the right way for you: that is divine law. *One is Truth*: true Reality transcends the boundaries of our beliefs. *Thou art That*: you are in the divine essence; you must be dedicated to fully realizing it.

Our religion may be right for us, nevertheless that does not mean billions of others are wrong. What of the

100 billion[*] people who lived outside of our faith since the origin of our species? Religions differ in approach, beliefs and practices, although the divine Reality they seek is the same. Their mystics used the words and concepts understood by followers of their faith, but these are just alternate ways of trying to express the One underlying Truth.

Divine union must be sought in this life, even for those believers in many lives. We cannot simply wait for death to bring us to the divine; waiting may result in our losing everything which we seek.

> Note: In Hinduism, "jiva" is a soul identified with the ego self; "atman" is the true Self or soul identified with Brahman. In some of the traditions of mysticism, a soul might have many aspects; in these essays, the word "soul" is only used in its divine aspect.

---

[*] See Wikipedia on the Internet for surprising historical statistics on "World Population."

Prominent Mystics

FEW MYSTICS WROTE books or had their teachings recorded by others; fewer yet were published and are available today. There have been millions of mystics, but some are especially well known for their leadership, writings or teachings.

Judaism, Christianity, Islam

Some prominent mystics of Judaism
(add ca. 3761 years for the Jewish calendar)
[23 quotes from 17 mystics]

Abraham ben Samuel Abulafia (1240–ca. 1291)
  Spanish kabbalist. Wrote *Light of Intellect* and other essays. ❖

Joseph ben Ephraim Caro (1488–1575)
  Rabbinic authority. Wrote *Beit Yosef (House of Joseph)*, code of Jewish law. ❖

Moses Cordovero (1532–70)
  Spanish kabbalist. Wrote *Orchard of Pomegranates, Precious Light*, etc. ❖

Dov Baer of Lubavitch (1774–1827)
  Russian Hasidic kabbalist. Son of Shne'ur Zalman. Wrote *Tract on Ecstasy.* ❖

Dov Baer of Mezhirech (d. 1772)
  Hasidic leader and kabbalist scholar. Teachings in *Maggid Devarav le-Ya'aqov.* ✽

Eleazar ben Judah of Worms (ca. 1165–1230)
  German scholar. Wrote *Roke'ah* and *The Secret of Secrets.* ✽

Isaac the Blind (ca. 1160–1235)
  Described as 'the father of the Kabbalah'; wrote commentary to *Sefer Yezirah.*

Israel ben Eliezer [Ba'al Shem Tov] (1700–60)
  Founder of East European Hasidism (criticized for "enthusiasm"). ✽

Abraham Isaac Kook (1865–1935)
  From Latvia; Ashkenazi Chief Rabbi of Israel. Wrote *The Lights of Holiness.* ✽

Isaac ben Solomon Luria [the Ari] (1534–72)
  Egyptian kabbalist. Wrote commentary on *The Book of Concealment.* ✽

Moses ben Shem Tov de Leon (ca. 1240–1305)
  Spanish kabbalist. Wrote *Mystical Midrash,* foundation for the Zohar. ✽

Rebi Nahman of Bratslav (1772–1811)
  Controversial Ukrainian zaddick. Followers are called "the dead Hasidism." ✽

Philo of Alexandria (ca. 10 BCE–50 CE)
  Hellenistic Jewish philosopher (reconciled early Greek and Jewish teachings). ✽

Shne'ur Zalman of Lyady (1745–1813)
  Founder of Habad Hasidism. Wrote *Likkutet Amarim,* its principle text. ✽

Simeon Bar Yohai (2nd C.)
  Moses de Leon atributed the *Zohar* to him (central writings of the Kabbalah). ❖

Hayyim ben Joseph Vital (1542–1620)
  Syrian Jewish kabbalist. Wrote *Tree of Life* and *The Book of Visions.*

❖ Quoted. Also quoted: Martin Buber, Shmelke of Nikolsburg, and Yehiel Mikhal of Zlotchov.

Some prominent mystics of Christianity
(BCE/CE, Common Era, are BC/AD)
[23 quotes from 20 mystics]

Saint Thomas Aquinas (ca. 1225–74)
  One of the greatest Catholic theologians (gained union very late in his life). ❖

Saint Athanasius (ca. 296–373)
  Bishop of Alexandria; church father. Wrote *On the Incarnation; Life of Antony.* ❖

Saint Augustine of Hipo (354–430)
  Convert from Neoplatonism (mystical insights and later doctrines conflicted). ❖

Augustine Baker (1575–1641)
  Influential Benedictine (English exile). Wrote *Holy Wisdom (Sancta Sophia).* ❖

Saint Bernard of Clairvaux (1090–1153)
  Monastic reformer and mystical writer (Cistercian abbot and crusader). ❖

Jakob Boehme (1575–1624)
  German Lutheran writer. Claimed direct divine inspiration for *Aurora.*

Saint Catherine of Genoa (1447–1510)
  Worked in a hospital in Genoa. Wrote *Dialogues on the Soul and the Body.* ❖

Dionysius [Pseudo-Dionysius](ca. 500)
  Converted by Paul [Syrian monk?] Wrote *Mystical Theology* among others. ❖

Meister Johannes Eckhart (ca. 1260–1327)
  German theologian/preacher of Dominican Order. Extremely influential. ❖

George Fox (1624–91)
  (English) founder of the Society of Friends (Quakers). Wrote his *Journal.* ❖

St. Gregory I 'the Great' (ca. 540–604)
  Elected Pope from 590. Wrote *Pastoral Care, Commentary on Job* and others.

Saint Gregory of Nazianzus (329–89)
  Cappadocian father. Wrote *Theological Orations* and *Philocalia of Origen.* ❖

Saint Gregory of Nyssa (ca. 330–95)
  Cappadocian father. Wrote *Catechetical Orations, Life of Moses* and others. ❖

Saint Gregory Palamas (ca. 1296–1359)
  Greek Orthodox archbishop. Wrote *Triads in Defence of the Holy Hesychasts.*

Bede Griffiths (1907–93)
  Benedictine monk; prior of ashram in India. Wrote *Marriage of East and West.* ❖

Hildegard of Bingen (1098-1179)
  Benedictine abbess, writer, composer, philosopher, mystic, and visionary.

Saint John of the Cross (1542–91)
  Founder of the Discalced Carmelites. Wrote *Dark Night of the Soul* and others. ❖

Nicholas of Cusa (ca. 1400–64)
  German Christian philosopher; made a cardinal. Wrote *De Docta Ignorantia.* ❖

Saint Jan van Ruysbroek [Ruusbroec] (1293–1381)
  Flemish Christian mystic. Wrote *The Spiritual Espousals.* ❖

Henry Suso (ca. 1295–1366)
  German Dominican monk. Wrote *Little Books of Truth and Eternal Wisdom.* ❖

Saint Symeon the New Theologian (949–1022)
  Byzantine mystic; Abbot at St. Mamas in Constantinople (Istanbul). ❖

Saint Teresa of Avila (1515–82)
  Spanish Carmelite abbess. Wrote the *Interior Castle* and her *Autobiography* ... ❖

Saint Tikhon of Zadonsk (1724–83)
  Russian Orthodox bishop and mystical writer (revered by Dostoevsky).

❖ Quoted. Also quoted: Angela of Foligno, Maximus the Confessor and Simone Weil.

Some prominent mystics of Islam
(subtract ca. 622 years for the Islamic calendar)
[23 quotes from 19 mystics]

Abd al-Karim al-Jili (ca. 1365–1412)
  Mystic (taught in Baghdad). Wrote *The Perfect Man*, referring to Muhammad.

Abu Yazid al-Bistami [Bayazid of Bistun] (d. 875)
  Persian ascetic (saint). Wrote nothing, but much quoted by Sufis. v

Abu Hamid Muhammad al-Ghazali (1058–1111)
  Master of jurisprudence. Wrote *Revival of the Religious Sciences.* ❖

Abu 'l-Mughith al-Husain b. Mansur al-Hallaj (857–922)
  Controversial Iraqi Sufi (saint). Wrote *Kitab al-Tawasin.* ❖

Abu 'l-Qasim al-Junaid (d. 910)
  (Saint) Laid the foundations for much of the development of "sober Sufism."

Farid al-Din Attar (d. 1229)
  Persian mystical poet. Wrote *Language of Birds, Divine Book* and others.

Dhu'l-Nun al-Misri (d. 859)
  Egyptian spiritual head of Sufis of his time. Leading authority on ma'rifa. ❖

Hajji Bektash Vali (12th C.)
  Founder of Turkish Derwish order, controversial Shi'ite sufi. ❖

Hasan al-Basri (632–728)
  One of the influential Sufis, regarded third master after Muhammad and 'Ali.

Muhyi al-Din Ibn (al-)'Arabi (1165–1240)
  Great Sufi (saint). Wrote *Meccan Revelations, Bezels of Wisdom,* etc. ❖

Sir Muhammad Iqbal (1876–1938)
  Poet of Lahore (saint). Wrote *Reconstruction of Religious Thought in Islam.*

Jalal al–Din Rumi [Mawlana] (1207–73)
  Great mystic poet (saint). Wrote *Poems of Shams-i-Tabriz* and many others. ❖

Mawlana Nur al-Din 'Abd al-Rahman Jami (1414–92)
  Afghan Sufi poet. Wrote *The Seven Thrones* among many others. ❖

Rabi'a al-Adawiyya (ca. 713–801)
  Outstanding female Sufi (saint) (important proponent of selfless love of God). ❖

❖ Quoted. Also quoted: Hazreti 'Ali, Khwaja Mir Dard, Hazrat Inayat Khan, Pir Vilayat Inayat Khan, Nawab Jan-Fishan Khan, Abu-Sai'd Abi'l Khayr, Sharafuddin Maneri, Rauf Mazari, Pahlawan-i-aif, and Mahmud Shabestari.

> Note: Listings were extracted from the Oxford Concise Dictionary of World Religions.

Hinduism, Buddhism

All Hindus and Buddhists should follow the mystical quest and most believe in divine law, divine justice, rebirth, and eventual liberation, but their approach and doctrines are very different, with many variations among their schools.

Some prominent mystics of Hinduism
(this aeon, or yuga, began 3102 BCE)
[23 quotes from 12 mystics]

Abhinavagupta (960–1050)
  Theologian of Kashmir Shaivism. Wrote *Light on Tantra* and on aesthetics.

Anandamayi Ma [Nirmala Sundari Devi] (1896–1982)
  She attained union at age 18 without aid of scriptures or guru. *

Sri Aurobindo [Aurobindo Ghose] (1872–1950)
  Founded ashram in Pondicherry. Wrote *The Life Divine* and others. *

Badarayana (1st C. BCE/4th C. CE)
  First propounded the basic teaching of Vedanta in the *Bhramasutra*.

Basava [Basavanna] (ca. 1106–67)
  Founder of Lingayata, known as Virashaivism. The body is the true temple.

Sri Krishna C(h)aitanya (ca. 1485–1533)
  (Maratha Saint) Major influence on development of devotion to Krishna.

Jnanesvar [Jnanadeva] (1275–96)
  At age 15 wrote *The Lamp of Plain Meaning*, revered in Marathi literature.

Kanada [Kanabhuj] (ca. 2nd C. BCE)
  Founded Vaisesika system. Developed atomic theory of nature.

Lalla [Lal Ded] (14th C.)
  Shaivite poetess. Her sayings are loved in Kashmir by Hindus and Muslims. *

Madhva [Madhvacarya] (ca. 1238–1317)
  Founder of Vaishnava school; proponent of dualism (dvaitavedanta).

Manikavacakar (ca. 9th C.)
  Tamil poet and Shaivite saint; one of Nayanmars. Wrote *Sacred Utterances*. *

Mirabai [Meera] (ca. 1498–1546)
  Unconventional woman whose songs of Krishna are popular in much of India.

Nimbarka (ca. 12th C.)
  Founder of Vaishnava sect; wrote commentary on the *Vedanta Sutra*.

Patanjali (ca. 2nd C.)
  Reputed author of the *Yoga Sutra*, a systematic presentation of classical yoga.

Sarvepalli Radhakrishnan (1888–1975)
  Hindu philosopher and President of India 1962–67. Wrote many books. ❖

Ramakrishna (1836–86)
  (Saint) Some English-educated Bengalis saw him as an avatar. ❖

Ramana Maharshi (1879–1950)
  Attained union at age 17. (Great saint of South India; idealized by Carl Jung). ❖

Ramananda (ca. 1360–1470)
  Founder of Vaishnavite Ramanandi (Maratha Saint); Kabir was his disciple.

Ramanuja (ca. 12th C.)
  Source of Visistadvaita-vedanta school, qualified non-dualism.

Ram(a)prasad (18th C.)
  Saint and poet of Bengal; devoted to Kali.

Ravi Das [Raidas] (ca. 15th C.)
  Saint and poet. The *Adi Granth* (Sikh scripture) contains 40 of his hymns.

Sahajanaanda Swami [Swaminarayan] (1781–1830)
  Follower of Ramanuja; regarded as an avatar of Vishnu.

Sai Baba of Shirdi (d. 1918)
  Some Hindus regarded him as an avatar (many Muslims consider him a saint).

S(h)ankara [Sankaracarya] (788–820)
  Proponent of Advaita Vedanta (monism). One of the most influential Hindus. ❖

Sankaradeva (1449–1569)
  Spread Vaishnava movement in Assam. Used music, dance and drama.

S(h)ivananda (1887–1963)
  (Exponent of Japa) Founder of the Divine Life Mission, branches worldwide. ❖

Sri Harsa (1125–80)
  Great logician. Wrote *Khandanakhandakhadya*. Method parallels Nagarjuna.

Tukaram (ca. 1607–49)
  Hindu poet (Maratha Saint). Wrote 7,000 verses, devotional and practical.

Tulsidas [Tulasidas] (1532–1623)
  Poet devotee of Rama (Maratha Saint). Wrote *Holy Lake of Deeds of Rama*.

Vallabha (1473–1531)
  Taught Suddhadvaita (non-duality) Vedanta; atman and Brahman are united.

Vidyaranya [Madhavacarya] (14th C.)
  Philosopher of Advaita Vedanta. Wrote *Pancadasi*, its basic work. ❖

Vivekananda (1863–1902)
Founded Ramakrishna Mission; taught Ramakrishna and Vedanta worldwide.

Paramahansa Yogananda (1893–1952)
Founder of Self-Realization Fellowship in the U.S.A. Advocated kriya-yoga.

❖ Quoted. Also quoted: Amritanandamayi Ma and Swami Nikhilananda.

Some prominent mystics of Buddhism
(adopts local calendars; time is insignificant)
[23 quotes from 20 mystics]

Asanga (4th C.)
Founded Yogacara/Vijnanavada school of idealism; wrote monumental works.

Asvaghosa [Ashvagosha] (2nd C.)
(Indian Mahayana philosopher) Wrote *The Acts of the Buddha* and others. ❖

Bodhidharma (5th C.)
Indian first patriarch of Ch'an in China. Emphasized dhyana (absorption). ❖

Buddhadasa (1905–1993)
Thai influential Buddhist scholar; removed myths from traditional beliefs.

Buddhaghosa (4th C.)
Wrote *The Way of Purity*, vital in understanding post-canonical Buddhism. ❖

Chinul (1158–1210)
Reformed Son (Ch'an); revitalized Buddhism in Korea. Integrated lineages.

Dalai Lama [Tenzin Gyatso] (b. 1935)
14th Dalai Lama dating from 1391. Won the Nobel Peace Prize in 1989.

Zenji Dogen Kigen (1200–53)
Founded Soto Zen in Japan. Wrote *The Treasury of the Eye of True Dharma*. ✧

Fa-Tsang [Hsien-shou] (643–712)
Third patriarch and major organizer of Hua-yen school of Chinese Buddhism. ✧

Huang-po Hsi-yun [Obaku Kiun] (d. 850)
Ch'an/Zen master. His teachings are in *Chu'an-hsin-fa-yao*.✧

Hui-neng [Eno] (638–713)
Sixth patriarch of Ch'an. Wrote *Platform Sutra*; depicted as tearing up sutras. ✧

Lin-chi I-hsuan (d. 867)
Outstanding Chinese master; founded the Zen Lin-chi line (Rinzai-shu).

Milarepa [Mi-la Ras-pa] (1043–1123)
Instrumental in founding Kagyu; he remains exemplary to many Tibetans. ✧

Nagarjuna (ca. 150–250)
Founded Madhyamaka; very influential. Wrote *Mula-Madhyamaka-Karika*.

Ratnakarasanti [Santi] (11–12th C.)
Philosopher; wrote commentaries on *Perfection of Wisdom* sutras and others. ✧

Saicho [Dengyo Daishi] (767–822)
Japanese monk; founded Tendai. Wrote *Superlative Passages of Lotus Sutra*.

Santaraksita (705–88)
  Indian philosopher in Tibet. Wrote *Compendium of Reality* and others.

Santideva (8th C.)
  Poet of Madhyamaka. Wrote *Entering the Path of Enlightenment* and others. ❖

Seng-ts'an [Sosan] (d. 606)
  Third patriarch of Ch'an/Zen in China. Wrote *Inscribed on the Believing Mind.* ❖

Daisetz Taitaro Suzuki (1870–1966)
  Professor of Buddhist Philosophy. Known in the West for his writings on Zen. ❖

Te-shan Hsuan-chien [Tokusan Senkan] (782–865)
  After satori, burned his beloved writings on the Diamond Sutra. ❖

Tsong Khapa (1357–1419)
  Founded Geluk school in Tibet. Wrote *The Great Graduated Path* and others.

❖ Quoted. Also quoted: Lama Govinda, Hui-Hai, Nisargadatta, Saraha, Shutaku, Shunryu Suzuki, and Yung-chia Ta'shih.

Note: Listings were extracted from the Oxford Concise Dictionary of World Religions

Mystic Viewpoints

THERE ARE MATTERS which are important within most religions' orthodoxy, to their leaders and to many followers, but are viewed differently by mystics. Mysticism often interprets them based on their effects in aiding or impeding search for union with the divine.

Evil and deliverance: Many orthodox religions personify evil as Satan, the Devil, Iblis, Mara, or other demonic forces. Most mystics hold us responsible for our own evils, not an external source. Some say that evil exists only in rejection or lack of awareness of good, or to balance good in the apparent dualities of this life ... not in unitive eternal life. Mystics have to eliminate personal wrongs to realize divine oneness. Deliverance comes by overcoming the selfishness of our egos, ignorance of our minds and stubbornness of our senses.

Sin and atonement: Christianity believes humans are born in sin because of the fall of Adam. Sin within Islam is an offense against God; in Judaism it is rejecting God's will. Buddhism and Hinduism believe that the consequences of sin can be carried over from our past life. Most mystics say that each of us is born with the essence of the divine; sin is our separation from the divine, ignoring or not seeking our soul. Mystics view atonement as accepting at-one-ment; it is reuniting with our soul and the One divine essence in All.

Messiahs and salvation: Messiahs are said to be those who can liberate or save their faithful. Buddha, Jesus, Krishna, and Rama in their religion may be considered messiahs. Many within Judaism believe that a future messiah will bring God's kingdom to Earth to save its people. Few mystics had claimed to be messianic and most rejected such claims by their followers. We must liberate ourselves by transcending our self; our salvation is actualizing divine union.

Prophets, messengers and incarnations: Buddhist mystics may venerate Buddha, arhants, bodhisattvas, or others who had realized or neared enlightenment. Christian mystics are devoted to Jesus Christ and admire the apostles who spread his Word. Hindu mystics adhere to teachings of Krishna, Rama and/or other manifestations of Brahman. Islamic mystics said that Muhammad was the Perfect Man, who taught the secret of true Reality underlying Allah. Jewish mystics are in awe of Moses as their paragon and honor many other biblical prophets. Although mystics revere these perfect exemplars, most believe that each person must seek their own unity with the divine, perhaps with guidance from teachers in this life.

Allah, Buddha, God, ha-Shem, Ishvara: Most religious people worship a personal deity, a non-theistic ideal or an intermediary. Unlike most of those in the mainstream, faith alone is not sufficient for mystics. They expanded to a search for oneness with the divine essence. Mystics, and later their followers, sought an underlying Reality, or divine ground, which some may call al-Haqq, Brahman, Dharmakaya/Nirvana, Ein Sof, Godhead, or other words. It is *One*: transcendent to and immanent in all existence; the absolute nature of being itself. Their "faith" is that union is possible during this life.

Grace: Divine grace is spiritual assistance not specifically earned by its recipient. Most mystics believe that divine grace is offered at all times, in all places and to all beings, but the sentiments, thoughts and actions of the ego self, and individual isolation, block its entry. Everyone has received divine grace during selfless periods of their life. Mystics who gave up their ego and individuality were in a state of grace and may share it. Most mystics say that grace is essential to realize oneness; some seem to equate divine grace, love and spirit.

Ritual and symbols: The *inner* meanings of the scriptures, the *spiritual* teachings of the prophets and personal searchings which can lead to divine union were often given lesser importance than outward rituals, symbolism and ceremony in many institutional religions. Observances, reading scriptures, prescribed acts, and following orthodox beliefs cannot replace your personal dedication, contemplation, activities, and direct experience. Preaching is too seldom teaching. For true mystics, every day is a holy day. Divine revelation is here and now, not limited to sacred scriptures.

Conflicts in conventional religion: *What's in a Word?* outlined some primary differences between religions and within each faith. The many divisions in large religions disagreed, sometimes bitterly. The succession of authority, interpretations of scriptures, doctrines, organization, terminology, and other disputes have often caused resentment. The customs, worship, practices, and behavior within the mainstream of religions frequently conflicted. Many leaders of any religion had only united when confronted by someone outside their faith, or by agnostics or atheists. Few mystics have believed divine oneness is exclusive to their religion or is restricted to any people.

> Note: This is just a consensus to indicate some differences between the approaches of mystics and that of their institutional religion. These statements do not represent all schools of mysticism or every division of each faith. Whether mystical experiences vary in their cultural context, or are similar for all true mystics, is less important than that they transform each one's sense of being to a transpersonal outlook on all life.

Quotations of Mystics

Orthodox Spirituality
By a Monk of the Eastern Church. Published by St. Vladimir Seminary Press 1945, 1987

" ... essential foundations of Orthodox spirituality. The aim of man's life is union with God (henosis) and deification (theosis). The Greek Fathers have used the term 'deification' to a greater extent than the Latins. What is meant is not, of course, a pantheistic identity, but a sharing, through grace, in the divine life. Union with God is the perfect fulfillment of the 'kingdom' announced by the Gospel, and of that charity or love which sums up all the Law and Prophets. 'We are made sons of God' says St. Athanasius."

"The distinction between persons does not impair the oneness of nature, nor does the shared unity of essence lead to a confusion between the distinctive characteristics of the persons. Do not be surprised that we should speak of the Godhead as being at the same time unified and differentiated ... diversity-in-unity and unity-in-diversity."
St. Gregory of Nyssa (C)

The Enlightened Mind
Edited by Stephen Mitchell. Published by HarperPerennial/ HarperCollins 1991, 1993

"Great knowledge, round and clear, looks at a fine hair and comprehends the ocean of nature; the source of reality is clearly manifest in one atom, yet illumines the whole being. When myriad phenomena arrive, they must be at the same time, in one space; noumenon [spiritual essence] has no before or after." Fa-Tsang [Hsien-shou] (B)

"We may compare it to a mirror which, though it doesn't contain any forms, can nevertheless reflect all forms. Why? Because it is free from mental activity. If your mind was clear, it wouldn't give rise to delusions, and its attachments to subject and object would vanish; then purity would arise by itself, and you would be capable of such perception." Hui-Hai (B)

Note: (720–814) Established Chan/Zen monastic rules.

"What formerly was hearsay now becomes known to you intuitively as you contemplate the works of God. Then you entirely recognize you do not have the right to say 'I' or 'mine.' At this stage you behold your helplessness; desires fall away from you and you become free and calm. You desire what God desires; your own desires are gone ..." Abu-Sai'd Abi'l Khayr (I)

Note: (967–1049) Persian mystic and poet. His practice was service to the poor.

"To study Buddhism is to study the self. To study the self is to forget the self. To forget the self is to be enlightened by all things. To be enlightened by all things is to drop off our body and mind, and to drop off the bodies and minds of others." Zenji Dogen Kigen (B)

"When you lose yourself in God, you proclaim the divine unity. Lose the sense of 'being lost'—that is complete detachment." Sharafuddin Maneri (I)

Note: (1263–1381) Indian Sufi.

"Love your neighbor like something which you yourself are. For all souls are one. Each is a spark from the original soul and this soul is wholly inherent in all souls, just as your soul is in all members of your body." Shmelke of Nikolsburg (J)

Note: (d. 1778) Moravian rabbi.

" ... so there is nothing in the world but the Creator, blessed be he. This is the opposite of what people imagine; when they are not attached to God but to earthly things, they think that they exist, and they are great in their own eyes. But if, out of love for God, they think they are nothing, and cleave to him with all their mental powers, they are very great, since the branch has come to the root and is one with the root." Yehiel Mikhal of Zlotchov (J)

Note: (1726–1781) Ukrainian Hassidic rabbi.

" ... most beautiful and profound emotion we can experience is the sensation of the mystical. It is the sower of all true science. To know that what is impenetrable to us really exists, manifesting itself as the highest wisdom and most radiant beauty—which our dull faculties can comprehend only in their primitive form — this knowledge, this feeling, is at the center of all religion." Albert Einstein (J)

Note: His theories of relativity revolutionized physics (not a mystic).

"God's grace is the beginning, middle and the end. When you pray for God's grace, you are like someone standing neck deep in water and yet crying for water."
Ramana Maharshi (H)

"God continually showers the fullness of his grace on every being in the universe, but we consent to receive it to a greater or lesser extent." Simone Weil (J/C)

Note: (1909–43) Born Jewish, involved in Catholic Christianity, but never baptized, she has been called "a Saint outside the Church."

Note: Quotations relate to the summary as a whole, rather than to any one essay.

The Divine Is Not ...

SCRIPTURES, THEOLOGIANS and many religious leaders tell us what the divine *is* by listing grandiose attributes. Most mystics worship personal aspects of the divine *essence*, but they also speak of what it is not. Many of them said that the divine essence is nothing, i.e. *no thing*, that it is immanent in all things, yet is transcendent to everything. Mystics consider this seeming paradox to be a positive negation.

Avidya, non-knowledge in Sanskrit, is used in Buddhism for our "spiritual ignorance" of the true nature of Reality. *Bila kaif*, without knowing how in Arabic, is Islam's term for "without comparison" to describe Allah. *Ein Sof*, without end in Hebrew, is the "infinite beyond description" in the Kabbalah. *Neti, neti*, not this, not this in Sanskrit, refers to "unreality of appearances" to define Brahman. In *via negativa*, the way of negation in Latin, God is "not open to observation or description."

The divine does not have the imperfections or dichotomies which affect we humans in apparent realities: no gender, beyond relative good and evil, neither human nor non-human, not this, that or any other. The Bible says we were created in the image of God, which is true, yet incomplete. All existence emanated in the *spiritual image* of the divine. The divine is not anthropomorphic, i.e. does not have human qualities, still it is present in all people through its essence. Humans are most capable of consciously sharing in that essence.

Many mystics and some religions, in particular Buddhism and Islam, refer to the divine as absolute Truth, ultimate Reality. Some mystics equate grace, love and spirit with the divine essence. It is not even accurate to state that the divine exists, just that it *is*. The ineffability of the divine precludes any explanation which rational thought can understand. It is a mystery which our minds cannot solve.

Mysticism emphasizes spiritual *knowing*, which is not rational and is independent of reason, logic or images. *Da'at* is Hebrew for "the secret sphere of knowledge on the cosmic tree." *Gnosis* is Greek for the "intuitive apprehension of spiritual truths." *Jnana* is Sanskrit for "knowledge of the way" to approach Brahman. *Ma'rifa* in Arabic is "knowledge of the inner truth." *Panna* in Pali is "direct awareness"; perfect wisdom. These modes of suprarational knowing, perhaps described as complete intuitive insight, are not divine oneness; they are actualizing our inherent abilities to come closer to the goal. It is consummate cognition, unmediated discernment, with certainty.

Direct experience in the divine essence also has various names. *Devekut*, cleaving or being joined in Hebrew, is the immediate state of attachment or adhesion to God. Realizing the *Dharmakaya*, dharma-body in Buddhist Sanskrit*, is a consciousness of ultimate

---

* In Mahayana and Vajrayana; "satori" in Zen in Japan has similar connotations.

Reality void of dualities. *Fana*, annihilation or dissolution in Arabic, is achieved by extinguishing selfhood until all is Allah. *Samadhi*, putting together or union in Sanskrit, is the absorption of consciousness in Brahman. *Unio mystica*, mystical union in Latin, is an experience in which the soul of a human is said to enter into unity with God. These are the supreme experiences in this life; there are also alternate definitions and terms.

What happens when our performance in this play of life is over? Life after death was a subject for some scriptures and theologians, although religious leaders usually avoid commenting. The goal of most mystics—some say the eventual goal of all humanity—has a variety of names. *Baqa*, remaining in God in Arabic, is eternal life. *Moksha*, release from the cycle of birth and rebirth in Sanskrit, is total spiritual liberation. *Nirvana*, complete cessation of desires and attachment, is the final exit from this world of becoming. Few of the mystics of Christianity and Judaism use their orthodox religion's concepts of immortality or resurrection. It is return to the source. The names may vary; the Reality does not.

Mysticism is the great quest for the ultimate ground of existence, the absolute nature of being itself. True mystics transcend apparent manifestations of the theatrical production called "this life." Theirs is not simply a search for meaning, but discovery of what *is*, i.e. the Real underlying the seeming realities. Their objective is *not* heaven, gardens, paradise, or other celestial *places*. It is not being where the divine lives, but to be what the divine essence is here and now.

The divine is neither "up there" nor "down here"; it is not outside nor is it inside; it is at the infinite here.

The divine is neither before birth nor after death; it is not yesterday, today nor tomorrow; it is in the eternal now. There is no place where the divine is not, there is no time when the divine is not, because the divine is not related to space or time. The divine *is*; all other words are insufficient.

Some say that there are endless possibilities for what it is not. That is not true. The known Universe is finite and, although vast, it is limited. The divine is infinite with limitless possibilities.

> Note: Some believe the Universe itself is infinite and eternal, a continuum of expansion and contraction. Some physicists say that there are dimensions beyond space-time.

Mysticism Is Not ...

MANY PEOPLE, INCLUDING some leaders of Western religions, think that mysticism is either nonsense, heretical or both. They are only partially correct, may just misunderstand, or refuse to accept it.

Mysticism is non-sense; the experiences of mystics can neither be perceived nor measured. The empirical certainty of divine union can neither be verified nor refuted by *current* science. Many scientists today have no doubt that ultimate Reality does exist, although they are unable *as yet* to confirm it. Proven or unproven, Reality is what it is, whether we would rather believe, think or desire otherwise.

To say the soul is united with the divine does not deny supremacy of the divine, any more than a ripple can reject the greatness of its ocean. Mysticism may seem *pantheistic* "The divine is in all," *theistic*, "but all are not yet in the divine," *polytheistic*, "It is called by many names," and *non-theistic*, "but One underlies the many." Most of the mystics were *panentheistic*: the divine is within and beyond all, both immanent and transcendent. That view is not total heresy.

Some mystics in ancient history, and a few in modern times, had been denounced, banished or persecuted by their religion for their beliefs during their lifetime. Many of those same persons became recognized as inspirational leaders of their faith and have been idealized — some as saints — usually long after they had passed on.

Mystics are not demigods, even when they are in oneness with the divine. Most of them felt that miracles were distractions, although some have been attributed to them. Mystics occasionally appeared to be psychic, though that was frequently wordless communication between teacher and student. A few of them had seemed to instruct by their mere presence; many others had never taught at all.

Mysticism is not the supernatural occult. Divine Love, absolute Truth and ultimate Reality are not found in tea leaves, tarot cards or crystal balls. Mystics do not try to communicate with departed souls; they concentrated on uniting with their own soul. Meditation trances seek the divine, not past lives or the future. Neither palm readers nor numerologists can foresee your success in encountering it. In mystical consciousness, revelation is always here and now.

Divine union is not magic. Magicians may create illusions; mystics seek to remove them. The wizards of legends used magic for selfish gain; mysticism is a path to self(less) realization. Wicca uses *high magic* to connect a person's soul to a Goddess; mystics are neither warlocks nor witches. They do not belong to covens, cast evil spells nor perform sacrifices ... except their *self.* Their repetition of sacred words is for spiritual awareness, not for worldly powers.

Many religious people do believe in astrology, but most religions and mystics have rejected it (except

Hinduism and the Kabbalah). Divine essence is in the stars and planets, as it is in All, yet the stars and planets in any alignment do not make absorption in divine unity any easier nor more difficult. Awareness of this Universe and of universal oneness, however, are vital during the mystical quest.

Spirituality, unlike the occult spiritualism, is sometimes defined as an "attempt to grow in sensitivity to self, to others, to non-human creation, and to God who is both within and beyond this totality." In practice, spirituality will often "cultivate tranquility, mindfulness and insight, leading to virtues of wisdom and compassion." Most mystics are quite spiritual, yet not all spiritual people are mystics. True devotees of mysticism *should be* spiritual. In the *New Penguin Handbook of Living Religions*, within an extensive chapter on Spirituality, it says that "the term spirituality covers a wide range of religious orientations and experiences, whereas the different types of mysticism represent very specific spiritual experiences."

All mystical traditions, among all religions, in all eras, have had many common themes and beliefs, still they were not identical. Just as no two witnesses will testify to the same event in the same way, mystics' accounts of divine consciousness quite often differed. They usually interpreted spiritual input through their historical, cultural and personal situation. Similar or different, it changed their lives.

A few mystics seem to be always in divine union, many of them do return to it frequently, while most had unforgettable moments of oneness. As humans, all of them were subject to the limitations of words to express that for which no words are adequate. Each mystic had to form those inadequate words into the symbols and concepts which could be understood by people of their faith. Some may have modified their words to meet the personal needs of their followers, to avoid a conflict with their orthodox religion, and/or to clarify previous misunderstandings. Their experiences surpass any words.

Mysticism can be a bridge between religions. The search for the absolute and ultimate divine may be defined differently in Buddhism, Christianity, Hinduism, Islam, and Judaism, but the Reality itself is the same. Divine essence is universal; we must be aware of it.

> Note: Increased power of emotions, mind and body is incidental to spiritual realization. True mystics feel more deeply, think more clearly, and act more vigorously than most non-mystics.

Quotations of Mystics

The Perennial Philosophy
  Aldous Huxley. Published by HarperCollins 1944, 2004

"Supreme, beyond the power of speech to express, Brahman may yet be apprehended by the eye of pure illumination. Pure, absolute and eternal Reality: such is Brahman and 'Thou art That.' Meditate upon this truth within your consciousness." Shankara [Sankara] (H)

"The knower and the known are one. Simple people imagine they should see God, as if He stood there and they here. This is not so. God and I, we are one in [spiritual] knowledge." [Meister] Eckhart (C)

"Who is God? I can think of no better answer than, He is who is. Nothing is more appropriate to the eternity which God is. If you call God good, or great, or blessed, or wise, or anything else of this sort, it is included in these words, namely, He is." St. Bernard (C)

"The simple, absolute and immutable mysteries of divine Truth are hidden in the super-luminous darkness of that silence which revealeth in secret. For this darkness, though of deepest obscurity, is yet radiantly clear; though beyond touch and sight, it more than fills our unseeing minds with splendours of transcendent beauty."
Dionysius of Areopagite [Pseudo-Dionysius] (C)

"O Friend, hope for Him whilst you live, know whilst you live, understand whilst you live; for in life deliverance abides.

If your bonds be not broken whilst living, what hope of deliverance at death?

It is but an empty dream that the soul shall have union with

Him because it has passed from the body.
If He is found now, He is found then.
If not, we do but go to dwell in the City of Death." Kabir

Note: (d. 1518) He is a saint to Hindus, Muslims and Sikhs

"When not enlightened, Buddhas are no other than ordinary beings; when there is enlightenment, ordinary beings at once turn into Buddhas." Hui-neng (B)

"All that the imagination can imagine and the reason conceive and understand in this life is not, and cannot be, a proximate means of union with God."
St. John of the Cross (C)

"How shall I grasp it? Do not grasp it. That which remains when there is no more grasping is the soul."
Panchadasi [by Vidyaranya] (H)

"If thou shouldst say, 'It is enough, I have reached perfection,' all is lost. It is the function of perfection to make one know one's imperfection." St. Augustine (C)

"Mindfulness [attentiveness] should be strong everywhere, for mindfulness keeps the mind away from all distraction, into which it might fall and away from idleness."
Buddhaghosa (B)

From *Kabbalah — The Way of the Jewish Mystic*
Perle Epstein. Published by Shambhala Classics
1976, 2001 (J)

"All souls form but one unity with the Divine Soul. For God is the beginning and He is the end of all degrees of creation. And all the degrees are bound with His seal. He is the

unique Being, in spite of the innumerable forms in which He is clothed." Rabbi Simeon

"Think of yourself as nothing and totally forget yourself as you pray. Only remember that you are praying for the Divine Presence. You may enter the Universe of Thought; a state of consciousness which is beyond time. You must relinquish your ego." Maggid of Mezerich

"One who does not meditate [contemplate] cannot have Wisdom. One who does not meditate also does not realize the foolishness of the world. But one who has a relaxed and penetrating mind can see that it is all vanity."
Rebe Nachman [Nahman of Bratslav]

"Unify your heart constantly, at all times, at all hours, in all places, thinking of nothing except me, as I appear in my Torah and ritual. This is the mystery of unity, where a person yokes himself literally with his Creator. Your attitude toward everything in this world must be one of detachment ... unifying himself with his source completely."
Joseph Caro [Karo]

"Everything depends on the intensity of your concentration and your attachment on high."
The Ari [Isaac ben Solomon Luria]

Note: Quotations relate to the summary as a whole, rather than to any one essay.

To the Non-Religious

THESE ESSAYS AND quotations were directed to the more than five billion people who are active in, and/or identify with, some religion. There are at least one billion persons who are not religious.

Many truly religious people are bewildered by mysticism and some aggressively reject it because it upsets too many of their own cherished beliefs. Most mystics are deeply religious, but some of them, like Buddhists, do not believe in a soul or a Supreme Being. A few true mystics have no religion or religious faith: they speak of oneness, yet not with the divine. The other essays are from the perspective of those who do believe in a soul and a divine.

Each of us, whether religious or non-religious, has felt limitations of our bodies and of our minds. We all realize that our senses are restricted and our intelligence is not perfect. Some people, in their private moments, have resented the isolation of their individuality. For most of us, our egos refuse to accept death as *The End*. Many people want to believe they move on to heaven; many mystics feel that *"heaven"* is within us and must first be realized in life.*

---

* Divine Reality for most mystics is *not* heaven, paradise or other celestial *places*.

There are a multitude of realities beyond our own experiences and knowledge: the Internet, television, radio, reading, or listening to other people tell us that. Our awareness and understanding of all life on planet Earth is incomplete. Although we know this Universe does exist, we realize that it far exceeds our comprehension. What Reality is both within and beyond this Universe? Can we know it?

Many people cannot fully appreciate the lives of those who have much less — or much more — than they do: either financially, socially, physically, mentally, and/or in other characteristics. Humans cannot wholly understand the daily existence of other mammals, of sea creatures, of insects, or of seemingly insentient entities like trees, rivers and mountains. We seldom entirely comprehend our own self, let alone completely intuit the *inner self* of other beings.

Astronomers continue to seek signs of life outside Earth and most have no doubt that it exists. Many scientists find latent intelligence in the structure of matter and living organisms. Much of what had seemed impossible 100 years ago is commonly accepted today. The unknown, however, still far exceeds the known. There is another level of existence which each of us can discover. It is here and now.

We know that we are surrounded by many things which cannot be sensed. Radio waves, various forms of radiation, even the air we breath cannot be perceived unaided. There is also an essence — call it vital or spiritual — which permeates everything, yet transcends them all. How can we become aware of this universal essence and then consciously live within it? How will that change our life?

Mysticism, the belief in direct experience of the universal essence, has been reported to date back more than 3,000 years. The number of people who have realized union, however, has been quite a small percentage of all humans. Most are unwilling to make the necessary sacrifices and concerted efforts. Not many athletes ever earn an Olympic gold medal and relatively few persons have received a Nobel prize. Actualizing oneness in life is a greater achievement.

Two more quotations from *The Enlightened Mind* seem appropriate:

"The Tao is the law of nature, which you can't depart from even for one instant. Thus the mature person looks into his own heart and respects what is unseen and unheard. Nothing is more manifest than the hidden; nothing is more obvious than the unseen. Thus the mature person pays attention to what is happening in his inmost self."
Tzu-ssu (483–402 BCE)

Note: Grandson of Confucius, founder of a philosophy and doctrine of humanism ... unlike the religion of Taoism.

"Extensive as the 'external' world is it hardly bears comparison with the depth-dimensions of our inner being, which does not need even the spaciousness of the universe to be, in itself, almost unlimited. It seems to me, more and more, as though our ordinary consciousness inhabits the apex of a pyramid whose base in us ... broadens out to such an extent that the farther we are able to let ourselves down into it, the more completely do we appear to be included in

the realities of the earthly and, in the widest sense worldly [universal] existence, which are not dependent on time or space." Rainer Maria Rilke (1875–1926)

> Note: German-language poet, acknowledged as one of the greatest of the 20th century.

All of us know many surface realities of this world. There is within each of us a deeper Reality which is truly universal, in which all existence is united and that is accessible to any person dedicated to experiencing it. Many people call this *soul*, which is united with what most call *God*, although neither can be correctly named or described. These essays use the approach of mystics of five of the largest religions, but the search is open to everyone.

> Note: Ultimate Reality is beyond rational knowing: "avidya" (B), "bila kaif" (I), "Ein Sof" (J), "neti, neti" (H), "via negativa" (C), and other terms for the limits of our minds.

Quotations of Mystics

The Life Divine
  Sri Aurobindo. Published by E.P. Dutton & Co.
  1949, 2006 (H)

"The divine soul will be aware of all variation of being, consciousness, will and delight as the outflowing, the extension, the diffusion of that self-concentrated Unity developing itself, not into difference and division, but into another, an extended form of infinite oneness."

"The Divine Being [Brahman] is at once impersonal and personal: it is an Existence and the origin and foundation of all truths, forces, powers, existences, but it is also the one transcendent Conscious Being and All-Person of whom all conscious beings are the selves and personalities; for He is their highest Self [soul] and the universal indwelling Presence."

Foundations of Tibetan Mysticism
  Lama Govinda (1898–1985). Published by E.P. Dutton & Co. 1959, 2002 (B)

"In states of rapture, trance and highest intuition, as characterized by the stages of deep absorption in meditation, we experience the Dharmakaya as the luminous form of purely spiritual perception — as pure, eternal principles of form, freed from all accidentals — or as the exalted visions of higher reality."

"To the enlightened man, whose consciousness embraces the universe, the universe becomes his 'body', while his physical body becomes a manifestation of the Universal Mind, his inner vision an expression of the highest reality, his speech an expression of eternal truth ... "

"As soon as the Thought of Enlightenment takes root in him, the miserable one who was fettered by his passions to the prison of existence, becomes a son of the Buddhas. He become worthy of veneration in the world of men and gods." Santideva

The Way of the Sufi
Idries Shah. Published by E.P. Dutton & Co. 1970, 1990 (I)

"The Sufi who knows the Ultimate Truth sets and speaks in a manner which takes into consideration the understanding, limitations and dominant concealed prejudices of his audience. To the Sufi, worship means knowledge. Through knowledge he attains sight. The Sufi abandons the three "I's. He does not say 'for me', 'with me', or 'my property'. He must not attribute anything for himself." Ibn El-Arabi

"Seeking truth is the first stage toward finding it. After seeking comes the realization that Truth is also seeking the Seeker himself. The third stage ... in which the Sufi is learning from the Way, is when learning reaches a special stage: when the Seeker realizes he is acquiring knowledge in a range beyond 'seeking' and 'finding' or 'being sought.'" Pahlawan-i-aif

"For him who has perception, a mere sign is enough. For him who does not really heed, a thousand explanations are not enough." Haji Bektash [Vali]

"Truth is a Way to Love, to Knowledge, to Action. But only those who can find real Truth can follow its Path as a Way. Others imagine that they may find Truth, even though they do not know where to seek it, since what they call truth is something less." Rauf Mazari

"What, asks the shallow mind, is the behavior of the Sufis, which marks them out for us as Masters? What are the forms of Exercises of which we may boast? What Path will make a suitable Path for me? What are the places which give birth to Teachers? What are the habits and assurances which bring man to Truth? Desist you fools! Before it is too late, decide: do you want to study appearance, or Reality?"
Nawab Jan-Fishan Khan (d. 1864)

The Spiritual Teaching of Ramana Maharshi
Forward C.G. Jung. Published by Shambala 1972, 2004 (H)

" ... there is no need for endless reading. In order to quiet the mind one has only to inquire within oneself what one's Self [soul] is; how could this search be done in books?"

" ... therefore, in order to achieve that state of Silence which is beyond thought and word, either the path of knowledge, which removes the sense of 'I,' or the path of devotion, which removes the sense of 'mine,' will suffice. So there is no doubt that the end of the paths of devotion and knowledge is one and the same."

Note: Quotations relate to the summary as a whole, rather than to any one essay.

Warnings!

MYSTICISM IS A spiritual journey anyone can begin, but few will complete in this life. It is a maze filled with false starts, dead ends and self-doubt. Both charlatans and deluded believers abound. It may be more successful for the strong; the weak can be easily misled.

There have been deceptive claims of mystical experience. Some were hallucinations of psychotics and others induced by psychedelic substances. Unfortunately, there were also the boastings of bloated egos and the lies of outright frauds. Some cults distorted mysticism.

Buddhism, Christianity, Hinduism, Islam, and Judaism all have rich mystical traditions. Other religions have had mystics among them. First learn about mysticism, in all of its aspects, in your own faith before choosing a course best for you. Only then should you begin to explore its practices and systems in different religions; you may find each has something positive to offer. It is not exclusive.

Divine union is a noble goal, but the Western religions are often skeptical of mysticism. Do not expect the leaders of your church, mosque, synagogue, or temple to support your efforts. If they do believe that you are truly serious, they may be able to introduce you to someone in your faith who can guide you or refer you to some literature which may be helpful. A few of them may discourage you.

Most mystical traditions recommend finding a spiritual teacher. The *acaryas* of Buddhism, *gurus* of Hinduism, *shaikhs* of Sufism in Islam, *zaddiks* of the Kabbalah in Judaism, and the masters of Christian mysticism taught according to the levels of dedication, abilities and awareness of each person. Your own teacher should be chosen carefully; those best qualified seldom take all who seek them; beware of those who accept any who are willing to pay.

Some people have read essays or poetry written by mystics of their faith, while others studied the mystical teachings of the world's religions. Devotees have attended lectures, workshops or retreats where mysticism was imparted to them. There are those who pray daily, meditate for a short time regularly or spend hours thinking of the divine. A few people have had life changing experiences which increased their spirituality. There are no short cuts or sure ways for realizing divine unity. To be in the soul is to be in the divine.

The greatest hindrance to awareness of divine union is you: your own previous beliefs, prejudices and misconceptions might cause judgments which will make learning the unfamiliar so difficult. The greatest source for divine oneness is you. It is you who must seek and find *your* soul: that shared spiritual essence in which all of existence is united in divine Reality. It is always here and now.

Unlike searching for exotic places at the other ends of the Earth, the divine is constantly present. This is one trip that you cannot carefully plan in advance. All of your research will only get you to the foothills of the mountain. It is you who must scale the precipices, avoid the chasms, adjust to the rare air at higher levels, and suffer the various pains of climbing. The summit awaits.

Most people who undertake the mystical quest rarely speak of it to others. Few of their family or friends would be supportive. You can seldom identify mystics, those who have already realized divine oneness, although you will usually notice spiritual qualities in them. Be suspicious of all who publicly declare that they are mystics or have communed with the divine; they may be genuine or impostors.

If you think that the divine, angels or departed ones are speaking to you in voices you can understand, you should seek professional counseling. Obsessions, even divine ones, can lead to psychiatric problems.[*] Confusion, however, is a natural part of every learning process. Sometimes it is better to suspend the search until your emotions and mind calm. Eternal Reality will always be there.

Few people personally know saints, mystics or other spiritually enlightened individuals who are conscious of the divine oneness in All. Most of our parents and mentors taught us about the separateness of gender, race, age, position, religion, and other facets of this life.

Every objective worth attaining does require some sacrifices and considerable effort. The greatest achievement in life, actualizing divine unity, necessitates a huge sacrifice: that of giving up your *self*. Discarding your ego

---

[*] Psychiatrists who say mysticism seeks to escape reality never sought divine Reality.

and abandoning individuality will take more effort than any previous task. It requires incredible courage to try and even more to persevere. Very few people come to it naturally.

Those who diligently seek divine union will become better people on Earth, more in harmony with the universal divine and better prepared for whatever comes after this life. Potential benefits far outweigh the risks and dedication essential to attaining these goals.

> Notes: "Teacher" is a misnomer; no one can "teach" how to be a mystic, they can only guide you along the path. Most mystics were quite skeptical of "visions," though some prophets and mystics are said to have had them. Mystical "seeing" is not of an image.

Quotations of Mystics

Mysticism
Evelyn Underhill. Published currently by KDP 1911, 2011

"All that is not One must ever suffer with the wound of Absence, and whoever in Love's city enters, finds but room for One and, but in Oneness, Union." Jami (I)

"Whatever share of this world Thou dost bestow on me, bestow it on Thine enemies, and whatever share of the next world Thou dost give me, give it to Thy friends. Thou art enough for me." Rabi'a (I)

> Note: The most famous female Sufi.

"My me is God, nor do I know my selfhood save in Him. My Being is God, not by simple participation, but by true transformation of my Being." St. Catherine of Genoa (C)

"The end of Sufism is total absorption in God ... but in reality it is but the beginning of the Sufi life, for those intuitions and other things which precede it are, so to speak, but the porch by which they enter." al-Ghazali (I)

" ... self-love and self-will (those poisons of our spirits) are abated, and in time and in a sort destroyed; and instead of them there enter into the soul the Divine love and Divine will, and take possession thereof." Augustine Baker (C)

"For the eyes of the soul behold a plenitude of which I cannot speak: a plenitude which is not bodily, but spiritual, of which I can say nothing."
Angela of Foligno (ca. 1248–1309) (C)

"God visits the soul in a way that prevents it doubting when it comes to itself that it has been in God and God in it and so firmly is it convinced of this truth ... " St. Teresa of Avila (C)

Essential Kabbalah: Heart of Jewish Mysticism
Daniel C. Matt. Published by Castle Books 1995, 1997 (J)

"It is impossible [to write about it] because all things are interrelated. I can hardly open my mouth to speak without feeling as though the sea burst its dams and overflowed. How then shall I express what my soul has received? How can I set it down in a book?" Isaac Luria

"The essence of divinity is found in every single thing — nothing but it exists. Since it causes every thing to be, no thing can live by anything else. It enlivens them; its existence exists in each existent. Do not attribute duality to God." Moses Cordovero

"The greater you are the more you need to search for your self. Your deep soul hides itself from consciousness. So you need to increase ... elevation of thinking, penetration of thought, liberation of mind — until finally your soul reveals itself to you. Then you find bliss ... by attaining equanimity, by becoming one with everything that happens, by reducing yourself so extremely that you nullify your individual, imaginary form." Abraham Isaac Kook

Radiant Mind
Edited by Jean Smith. Published by Riverhead Books / The Berkeley Publishing Group 1999 (B)

[Universal Mind / divine consciousness] "The pure Mind, the source of everything, shines forever and on all with the brilliance of its own perfection. But people of the world do

not awake to it. Blinded by their own sight, hearing, feeling, and knowing, they do not perceive the spiritual brilliance of the source-substance. If they would only eliminate all conceptual thought in a flash, that source-substance would manifest itself like the sun ascending through the void and illuminating the whole universe without hindrance." Huang-po

"Satori may be defined as an intuitive looking into the nature of things in contradistinction to the analytical or logical understanding of it. Practically, it means the unfolding of a new world heretofore unperceived in the confusion of a dualistically trained mind. ... all its opposites and contradictions are united and harmonized into a consistent organic whole. Satori can thus be had only through our once personally experiencing it." D.T. Suzuki

"The real world is beyond our thoughts and ideas; we see it through the net of our desires; divided into pleasure and pain, right and wrong, inner and outer. To see the universe as it is, you must step beyond the net. It is not hard to do; the net is full of holes." Nisargadatta

Note: (1897–1981) Considered the most famous teacher of non-dualism since Ramana Maharshi.

"Renunciation is not giving up the things of the world, but accepting that they go away." Shunryu Suzuki

Note: (1904–71) Japanese abbot who taught Zen in the U.S.A.

Note: Quotations relate to the summary as a whole, rather than to any one essay.

Reality Is One

DIVINE REALITY IS infinitely here and eternally now, not within the spatial or temporal constraints of earthly realities. No words can ever describe ultimate Reality, yet a single word might suffice: *One*. Some people call it omniscient, omnipotent and omnipresent; some mystics speak of the One* underlying the many, the Real within all and beyond any of the apparent real. It is what *is* here and now.

Using Allah, (celestial) Buddha, God, ha-Shem, Ishvara, or other words does not change the divine essence. Preeminent Reality is the holy One in All and All in the wholly One. Soul is simply a word for our spiritual essence, now separated from the ocean of Reality by a cloud of ignorance. Like rain, it does come from that ocean and it will eventually return to it. The billions of souls on Earth are just as ripples in the vastness of the universal One.

The personal, yet transcendent, divine which we worship is also immanent in all existence. The word Godhead, used by Christians in English, is al-Haqq in Islam, Brahman in Hinduism, Dharmakaya or Nirvana in Buddhism, and Ein Sof in the Kabbalah of Judaism. These

---

* "One" is a simple, all-encompassing word used by many mystics of most religions.

are some words for the essence of the divine One, which both penetrates and exceeds everything. Mystics unite with eternal Reality which *is*; mysticism speculates on why, how or what it is.

Pure Reality surpasses both our experience and knowledge. Few people truly realize the unity of the undifferentiated One. Among dualities of mundane existence, we credit positive attributes to the divine, but that assumes there are also negatives or opposites. True Reality has none of the imperfections and dichotomies which affect humans in apparent realities. It is the absolute nature of being.

Humans are able to see, hear, touch, smell, and/or taste only a bit of worldly realities at any given time. Our mind, through reasoning, learning, remembering, and imagining can extend far beyond the reach of our senses, but it too is limited mostly to the small part of Earth which we experience directly or through the vision of others. Our concept of this Universe is severely restricted. Astronomy is primarily mathematical projections of what little we can see and measure with telescopes, spectroscopes and other instruments.

Each person knows just one of every 10,000 things of this world. The entire mundane knowledge of all humans would understand only a minute portion of the unfathomable One. People believe this life's experiences are *reality*. All human experiences pale before the consummate Reality of the boundless One. The greatest of all our human hopes, dreams and aspirations are exceeded upon complete awareness of oneness with the ultimate ground of existence.

Time and space are relative. Earth is 4.5 *billion* years old and its size dwarfs any human body. Relatively, one human lifetime is just a speck and one mortal space is infinitesimal. People began to write only 5,500 years ago. This Universe is 13.7 billion years old and has at least 100 billion galaxies. Relatively, all recorded history is simply a moment and planet Earth is small. Divine Reality exists within and *is* beyond this Universe, unrelated to either time or space.

Soul is not limited to this life alone. "Is *my* soul eternal? Will it live next to the almighty One in heaven? Will *my* soul bond with the beloved One in peerless Reality?" That is your ego speaking. You want to retain your individuality while attaining supremacy to it. Clinging to your ego and individuality blocks you from your goal. Replace love of self with love of the divine, knowing "me" with knowing the true One in you, self-serving by selfless service.

The soul in each person also unites it with the spirit in all beings: animate or inanimate. To say that we humans are superior to birds, trees, rivers, or mountains is not to be aware of the divine essence in Nature which always surround us. To say that Earth is superior to all other planets, or that the Milky Way is superior to all other galaxies, is not to be aware of the divine glory of this Universe. The supreme One, in its everlasting unity, excels any of all: it is All.

Some feelings seem common to many mystics when on the verge of divine union. These are symbolic expressions, not of one person, and are felt simultaneously. The radiance of endless Love dissolved conflicts of the exterior world. Absolute Truth in intuitive insight replaced knowing through images and words. Ultimate Reality absorbed them and illusions of separate realities disappeared. The bliss of Oneness surpassed all the pleasures in earthly multiplicity. They were about to fully experience the divine unity of existence.

Dim the spotlight on your ego; illuminate the beacon of the soul. Turn your focus from the outward realities; aim inward to inherent Reality. Suspend conducting personal affairs; dedicate yourself to performing for the sacred One. Open all the gates wide for divine union. Lights, camera, action: Let your quest for the divine begin. The greatest achievement in life is an ongoing production.

> Note: The "celestial" Buddha, or "Sambhogakaya," is a Mahayana concept somewhat similar to "God" in other religions ... although most Buddhists would seldom admit to it.

Quotations of Mystics

Mysticism in the World's Religions
Geoffrey Parrinder. Published by Oneworld Publications
1976, 1996

"The One, the most precious, the Infinite, came down to earth; I did not despise his descent as Guru who appeared in grace." Manikka Vachakar [Manikavavcakar] (H)

"The road to Buddhahood is open to all. At all times have all living beings the Germ of Buddhahood in them." Ratnakarasanti (B)

"For all things are in Him and He is in all things: He is both manifest and concealed. Manifest in order to uphold the whole, and concealed for He is found nowhere." Zohar (J)

"Of course God is the 'wholly Other'; but He is also the wholly Same, the wholly Present. He is also the mystery of the self-evident, nearer to me than my I." Martin Buber (J)

Note: (1878–1965) Best known for his book *I and Thou*.

[on the diversity of religions] "The lamp is different, but the light is the same. Love alone can end their quarrel. Love alone comes to the rescue when you cry for help against their arguments." Rumi [Mawlana] (I)

Note: He gave music and dance important roles in Sufism.

Awakening
Pir Vilayat Inayat Khan (1916–2004). Published by Jeremy Tarcher/Putnam 1999, 2000 (I)

"The soul in its manifestation on the earth is not at all disconnected to the higher spheres. It lives in all the spheres, although it generally is only conscious of one level. Only a veil separates us. The seer's own soul becomes a torch in his hand. It is his own light that illuminates his path. It is just like directing a searchlight into dark corners which one could not see before." Hazrat Inayat Khan

Note: (1882–1927) Sufi master from India who brought Chishti Sufism to Europe and America in the early 1900's; he was the father of Pir Vilayat.

" ... grasping the inner meaning and essence of the illuminated beings who have appeared throughout the ages. Instead of attuning to the historical Jesus, we think instead of the Cosmic Christ, or Buddha Tathagata [Enlightened] instead of Siddharta Gautama. As has been stressed by virtually all major religions, whether Hinduism, Buddhism, Judaism, or Islam, the image of the prophet or a saint can only be a stepping-stone toward our direct relationship with the Divine ... in which one loses oneself in the Divine Consciousness."

Hinduism
Swami Nikhilananda (1895–1973). Published by
Ramakrishna-Vivekananda Center 1958, 1992 (H)

"Brahman is one and without a second, and can be regarded either from the phenomenal or from the transcendental point of view. When the sense-perceived world is regarded as real, Brahman is spoken of as its omnipotent and omniscient Creator, Preserver and Destroyer. But when the world is not perceived to exist, as for instance in deep meditation, then one experiences Brahman as the unconditioned Absolute ... One worships the conditioned Brahman in the

ordinary state of consciousness, but loses one's individuality during the experience of the unconditioned Brahman."

Personal deity vs. divine essence.

"The universal religion has no location in time or space. Its area is infinite, like the God it preaches. Krishna, Christ, Buddha, and Moses all have honored places in it. Its sun shines upon all spiritual seekers: Hindu, Christian, Buddhist, or Moslem. There is no room in it for persecution or intolerance. Recognizing the potential divinity of all men and women it devotes its entire force to aiding men to realize their true divine nature. The real universal religion is not a creed or doctrine; it is an experience. It is God-consciousness."

"The nearer we are to God, the closer we shall feel toward other religions. In God we all meet. In order to promote religious harmony, let us deepen our religious consciousness. Let us come nearer to God by following our respective faiths and not by jumping from one faith to another. Let the Hindu, the Moslem, the Christian, the Jew emphasize the spirit and not the letter of their scriptures, and all religious quarrels will stop. All religions are challenged today by a common enemy: the rising tide of skepticism and secularism."

Note: Swami Nikhilananda founded the Ramakrisna-Vivekananda Center in New York. He had privately tutored me during the summer of 1960, which eventually led to my receiving a Carnegie grant to study in India.

Note: Quotations relate to the summary as a whole, rather than to any one essay.

Preconditions to Learning

THE SPIRITUAL DISCIPLINES of devotion, knowledge, selfless service, and/or meditation are best taught by those who already mastered them. The best students are those who have already mastered their *self*, by discarding their ego and abandoning their individuality.

While you are feeling, thinking or acting with the selfish purposes of *I, me* or *my* you cannot realize divine union. These concepts bind you to the mundane world with your confusing personal emotions, the preconceptions of your mind and the restrictions of your senses. You must reach beyond the ego self to the underlying self: the soul.

Love for the divine must be selfless; it is never complete while it is simply *your* sentiment. Concentration on divine Truth is not total while it is just one thought in *your* mind. The divine Reality cannot be experienced by *your* senses; the senses find symbols, not essence. Divine Love, Truth and Reality flow as One into the soul, yet they are independent of *your* self. The soul is always here and now.

Like each of the spiritual disciplines, discarding your ego and abandoning individuality must usually be accomplished in stages. In only a few instances have any mystics achieved these goals easily or quickly. Others may provide guidance, but every person must do it alone.

The quest may seem lonely when considered *yours*; there is no loneliness in the divine. It is sharing in universal consciousness.

Some people seem to be naturally selfless. It is easy for them to give up their ego because they are so concerned with the well-being of others. These rare and wonderful persons, however, can seldom escape their own feeling of separateness as an individual.

Others want control and express their ego strongly, yet they often lose their individuality while performing tasks for the betterment of their team. Directing, or at least guiding, activities as a member of the team seems the best way to accomplish these objectives.

Unfortunately, there are those who find it almost impossible, and undesirable, to give up either their ego or their individuality. Any goal only seems important to them in terms of its effects on *I, me* or *my*. These selfish people just look to the benefits for themselves.

As teachers, mystics will gladly take on the selfless students, find those driven by ego to be a challenge, yet ignore the selfish as not worthy of instruction. The first are easily guided, the second require disciplined direction, but the third are hopeless unless they change.

A Jewish mystic asked a prospective student "When someone insults you, do you still feel injured? When you receive praise, does your heart expand with pleasure?" When he answered "yes" he was told to come back in a few more years. In the Bhagavad-gita (Song of God), Hinduism's ancient text, the Lord Krishna tells the despondent warrior Arjuna that he must do his duty. "The world is imprisoned in its own activity,

PRECONDITIONS TO LEARNING 77

except when actions are performed as worship of God. Therefore, perform every action sacramentally and be free of all attachments to results." You must forget yourself, your entire self, to succeed. "You" is then integrated into the One.

Discarding your ego and abandoning individuality do not simply mean being *unselfish*. Properly seeking divine oneness will require losing all awareness of *self*. Consciousness in divine unity, after selflessly following the spiritual disciplines, results in losing any sense of separateness of *other*. These unforgettable experiences are initially momentary, they may be repeated and extended, and they should then be actualized to transform every aspect of your life.

Some people think that the total absence of self means physical death. Rather, as many Christian mystics might say it: "I die in God; through me His will be done." Arhants had awakened to Nirvana in this life and will be free from rebirth; bodhisattvas,* however, "vow to attain enlightenment to save all sentient beings." *Fana* is the Sufi state of perfection, achieved by annihilation of all human attributes and self-hood until God is all; "to die before one dies." You must realize divine union in life; only the most selfless do so at death.

How can you suppress the influence of self? Start by excluding *I*, *me* and *my* from your vocabulary and your mind. Forsake anything which is generated by

---

* Bodhisattva concepts differ between Buddhist schools. In other religions, they may be similar to saints, prophets or angels, depending on which are compared. The goal of mystics is questioned; do we seek liberation for ourselves or for all humankind?

your selfishness or pride. Center all of your sentiments, thoughts and activities on others. In the face of blame or criticism, even if it is misplaced, do not become upset, hurt or angry. When complimented or praised, accept it graciously, but do not allow it to swell the ego. Begin to live in and for the divine.

Gradually, that *you* will begin to exist as an integral part of the greater whole. Your entire being — emotional, mental and physical — will identify with everything around you. You will surpass the limits of the *self* you know now. Experiencing will then come as intuitive insight rather than in the fragmented inputs of feelings, conceptions and perceptions. Life becomes enriched while living in the soul.

Quotations of Mystics

The Roots of Christian Mysticism
Oliver Clement. Published by New City Publications
1982, 1995 (C)

"You alone have been made in the image of the Reality that transcends all understanding, the likeness of imperishable beauty, the imprint of true divinity, the recipient of beatitude, the seal of true light. When you turn to him you become that which he is himself ... he dwells in you and moves within you without constraint." Gregory of Nyssa

"He actually contains in himself all beings, that which had no beginning and will have no end, beyond any notions of duration and nature that our intellect could form for itself. He enlightens the higher part of our being, provided it has been purified." Gregory Nazianzen

"The deified person, while remaining completely human in nature ... becomes wholly in God in both body and soul, through grace and the divine brightness of the beatifying glory that permeates the whole person."
Maximus the Confessor

Note: (ca. 580–662) Greek theologian.

An Idealist View of Life
Sarvepalli Radhakrishnan. Published by Jeremy P. Tarcher/ Putnam 1932, 2003 (H)

Note: He was the President of India 1962–67, Vice President 1952–62 and a Professor at Oxford University 1936–52. In 1962, I was introduced to Dr. Radhakrishnan by John Kenneth Galbraith, then the U.S. Ambassador to India.

[samadhi / absorption] *"It is a condition of consciousness in which feelings are fused, ideas melt into one another, boundaries are broken, and ordinary distinctions transcended. Past and present fade away into a sense of timeless being. Consciousness and being are not different from each other. In this fullness of felt life and freedom, the distinction of the knower and known disappears. The privacy of the individual self is broken into and invaded by a universal self which the individual feels as his own. The experience itself is felt to be sufficient and complete. It does not come in fragmentary or truncated form demanding completion by something else. It does not look beyond itself for meaning or validity."*

"It is the aim of religion to lift us from our momentary meaningless provincialism to the significance and status of the eternal, to transform the chaos and confusion of life to that pure and immortal essence which is its ideal possibility. If the human mind so changes itself as to be perpetually in the glory of the divine light, if the human emotions transform themselves into the measure and movement of the divine bliss, if human action partakes of the creativity of the divine life, if the human life shares the purity of the divine essence, if only we can support this higher life, the long labour of the cosmic process will receive its crowning justification and the evolution of centuries unfold its profound significance. The divinising of the life of man in the individual and the race is the dream of the great religions. It is the moksha of the Hindus, the nirvana of the Buddhists, [baqa of the Muslims] the kingdom of heaven of the Christians [the messianic age of the Jews]. It is the realization of one's native form, the restoration of one's integrity of being. Heaven is not a place where God lives but an order of being, a world of spirit where the ideas of wisdom, love

and beauty exist eternally, a kingdom into which we all may enter at once in spirit, which we can realize fully in ourselves and in society though only by long and patient effort. The world reaches its consummation when every man knows himself to be the immortal spirit, the son of God, and is it. Till this goal is reached, each saved individual [who has actualized divine union] is the centre of the universal consciousness. He continues to act without the sense of ego. To be saved is not to be moved from this world. Salvation is not an escape from life. The individual works in the cosmic process no longer as an obscure and limited ego, but as the centre of the divine or universal consciousness embracing and transforming into harmony all individual manifestations. It is to live in the world with one's inward being profoundly modified. The soul takes possession of itself and cannot be shaken from its tranquility by the attractions and attacks of the world."

"Intuitive insight ... is a whole view where the mind in its totality strains forward to know the truth. The realization of this undivided unitary life from which intellect and emotion, imagination and interest arise is the essence of the spiritual life. Ordinarily we are not whole men, real individuals, but wrecks of men, shells of individuals. Our responses are formal and our actions are imitative. We are not souls but human automata."

Note: Quotations relate to the summary as a whole, rather than to any one essay.

Love, Knowledge and...

SEEKERS OF SPIRITUAL knowledge might ask, "What's love got to do with it?" Devotees of devotion reply, "Divine love is everything." In mystical "marriage," divine union, you can't have one without the other. Divine Love and divine Truth are One in divine Reality.

In Sufism of Islam, knowledge is the key which opens the lock of love. *Ma`rifa*, spiritual knowledge, is essential to properly guide those who are intoxicated with *mahabba*, love for the divine. They are two of the last stations on the mystical path. Sufism often uses exquisite poetry to convey our longing for the divine. Some of the verses were considered too erotic by orthodox Muslim clerics. Sufis say that they are just allegories to express the inexpressible.

In Hinduism, *bhakti* is our devotion in love and adoration of the divine. *Jnana* is knowledge of the way to approach the divine. Both are considered paths to realize divine union and to be released from *samsara*, the cycle of birth and rebirth. The way of devotion is the preferred path of most Hindu movements, as in many orthodox religions; the way of knowledge is emphasized in Vedanta; *preferred* and *emphasized*, perhaps, but they are not mutually exclusive.

The "Song of Songs" (Song of Solomon) in the Hebrew Bible, or Old Testament, is a series of love poems which may appear to be secular. Both Jewish and Christian mystics, however, interpret them as love between God and us. The "mystical marriage" is mentioned frequently in the Kabbalah of Judaism and by Christian mystics, although the latter often allude to love between Jesus and his faithful. Divine union is the joining of the lover and beloved; it is also the unity of knower and known. Love and knowledge are coequal and complementary.

All Buddhists are devoted to the Buddha; many may also worship celestial bodhisattvas and/or *devas* (deities).* They do not "love the divine" in the common, theistic sense, but that which is found in highest spiritual experience. Sanskrit *prajna*, the direct awareness of *sunyata*, emptiness of self, is the perfect wisdom. Love is usually expressed as *loving kindness*, universal love for all beings ... a concept and virtue shared by the traditions of mysticism in all religions.

Most orthodox religions *and* their mystical tradition seem to like combinations of three, typically as aspects of the divine. These essays use Love, Truth and Reality as three perspectives of the divine One. Our being in this life also has three basic appearances: emotional, mental and physical. "Celestial spheres" of heaven, earth and hell are absent from many schools of mysticism. Most concepts italicized are unique to each faith, despite some similarities.

Mahayana and Vajrayana vehicles of Buddhism speak of *Trikaya*, or three bodies: *Nirmanakaya* is the Buddha in human form, *Sambhogakaya* is celestial Buddha and *Dharmakaya* is the formless essence, or Buddha-nature.

---

* Deities adopted from native religions, or transformations of Buddhas or bodhisattvas.

The Theravada primarily addresses the historic Buddha. The "Three Jewels" are the Buddha, the *dharma* (his teachings) and the *sangha* (the community of monks and nuns).

Christianity has its Trinity: Father, Son and Holy Spirit referring to God, Jesus Christ and their spiritual bond of unity (some say the Godhead). Interpretation of the essential nature of each, and their relationship, differed among the churches. In Christian mysticism, the three ways of the spiritual life are the *purgative* in being purified from sin, the *illuminative* in true understanding of created things, and the *unitive* in which the soul unites with God by love.

In the Kabbalah of Judaism, *sefirot*—sparks from the divine—have three fulcrums to balance the horizontal levels of the Tree of Life: *Da'at* (a quasi-sefirot) is knowledge combining understanding and wisdom; *Tiferet* is beauty, the midpoint of judgment and loving kindness; *Yesod* is the foundation for empathy and endurance. They also vertically connect through *Keter*, the supreme crown, the infinite and transcendent *Ein Sof* with its kingdom in the immanent *Shekhinah*.

Hinduism's *trimurti* are the threefold activities of Brahman: in Brahma as creator, in Vishnu as sustainer and in Shiva as destroyer. *Saccidananda* are the triune attributes or essence of Brahman: *sat*, being, *cit*, consciousness and *ananda*, bliss. The three major schools of yoga are *bhakti*, devotion, and *jnana*, knowledge—both described above—and *karma*, the way of selfless action. *Raja* yoga can apply to, and integrate, all three in mental and spiritual concentration.

In Islam, *nafs* is the ego-soul, *qalb* is heart and *ruh* is spirit. Heart is the inner self [soul], hardened when it is turned toward ego and softened when it is polished by *dhikr*, remembrance of the spirit of Allah. This is a three-part foundation for Sufi psychology. Initiation guides them from *shari`a*, religious law, along *tariqa*, the spiritual path, to *haqiqa*, interior reality. It is a gradual unveiling of the Real.

This life's mortal loves, mundane truths and worldly realities are finite and transient. In the divine One, endless Love, absolute Truth and ultimate Reality are infinite and eternal. It is what *is*.

> Note: Most Hindus worship one deity, chosen from the various aspects of Brahman.

Some Differences

MYSTICS' EXPERIENCES MAY be quite similar, still their techniques and interpretations had varied. Reading about mysticism in Buddhism, Christianity, Hinduism, the Kabbalah of Judaism, and Sufism of Islam, you will find many differences. In this life, people differ.

Schools of mysticism in each religion recognized that seekers had distinctive inclinations. Most aspirants respond best to devotional approaches, many of them were more contemplative*, some have preferred meditation,* while too few were primarily interested in helping others. The teachers often integrated these methods, yet tailored to the needs of individual devotees. No two are the same.

Qualified teachers have also realized that there were different motivations among their students. A few seemed to have been *born* spiritual, many came upon the quest later in life, perhaps due to an intense personal experience, and most of them just felt obligated — for diverse sociological and/or psychological reasons — to at least once attempt the search. Their dedication and abilities differed.

---

* The terms "contemplation" or "meditation" may mean the reverse (discursive vs. nondiscursive) in Eastern versus Western faiths. Discursive is a process of reasoning.

Mystics themselves were usually brought up with the symbolism, rituals and scriptures of that religion in which they had realized union. Their own mindset prior to an absorption in the divine may have influenced their later interpretation and, more likely, their recounting of it to others. The divine presence may then have been expressed in terms of a personal deity, a celestial image, a prophet, saint, or other figure familiar to them and/or to their followers.

The ultimate Reality of the divine One — its essence surpassing conception or perception — is absolute certainty for those absorbed in it. It had infused itself into every part of their being, confirming intuitive insight of, and increasing love for, the unity of all existence. Most mystics had then returned to their limited human self, many of them greatly transformed, but a few did continue in this universal consciousness for all the remaining years of their mortal life.

The theologies or philosophies — theosophy may be a better term except for a disputed movement using that name — of mysticism tried to rationalize a consciousness which was not rational. How do you explain the unexplainable? While it is impossible, that did not stop many mystics from trying to do it. Most of the controversies arose after their attempt. Some of them were just too confusing.

Techniques used to realize divine union have varied, too, not only between religions, but also among schools of mysticism in divisions of each faith. Students, although seldom the mystics themselves, often criticized other schools' approaches, while claiming that theirs was "the best." Perpetual mystics, those rare saints who had never left oneness with the divine, did not agree. They accepted that there were many paths which could reach the same goal.

The symbolism of mystics' orthodox faith, with references to its prophets and scriptures, frequently surfaced in both their writings and teachings. Although they may not have agreed with all aspects of their institutional religion, most mystics have felt that they were enhancing its wisdom and few believed they were being heretical. Because many mystics were criticized by leaders of their religion, or worse, they usually *tried* to conform to accepted depictions.

First concentrate on the mystical tradition of your religion: it too has alternative views. The *yogas* of devotional Shaivism, Shaktism and Vaishnavism, including their Tantrism, as well as the spiritual knowledge of Vedanta, have diverse schools. In the Kabbalah of Judaism, the early devotees of the Zohar were more esoteric than later, ecstatic Hasids. Buddhist *lamas* of Tibet, acariyas of the Theravada of Southeast Asia, and Zen masters of East Asia use distinctive techniques. The Christian mystics, of Eastern Orthodox Churches, Roman Catholics, Protestants, and especially Quakers, have dissimilar practices. The many Sufi orders of Islam, Shi'a and Sunni, may teach sober (gnostic), ecstatic and/or love mysticism.

Actual experiences in divine unity, assuming they were genuine, were often quite similar and varied primarily in degree, frequency and duration. Many mystics had read works of predecessors, both within and outside of their faith. Some had traveled to distant lands. Those perpetual mystics who did meet, regardless of their religion or nationality, could communicate without much conflict. They spoke amongst themselves unlike as they had to do with seekers.

Early mystics were mostly ascetics, monastics, religious teachers, or esoteric scholars. Modern mystics tend to be very involved in this world. Their universal perspective, lack of ego, spiritual tranquility, expansive attentiveness, and selfless service make them admired and respected members or leaders of both their organizations and communities. By awakening in the greatest achievement of this life, they may then consciously share in eternal oneness with the divine.

> Note: "Yoga" is a means or path to unite with Brahman. "Lamas" are spiritual teachers.

Primary Bibliography

Among all books referenced, these 100 were most useful in preparing *The Greatest Achievement in Life*. Most are available on Amazon.com by title and/or author; the 30 books quoted (❖) are especially recommended.

Buddhism

Buddhist Insight (Indo-Tibetan)
  Alex Wayman. Published by Motilal Banarsidass Publishers 1954, 2002

Essays in Zen Buddhism
  D.T. Suzuki. Published by Grove Press 1949, 2000 ❖

Foundations of Tibetan Mysticism
  Lama Anagarika Govinda [E. Hoffmann]. Published by Weiser Books 1959, 1999 ❖

Living Dharma: Teachings of 12 Buddhist Masters
  Jack Kornfield (Theravada). Published by Shambhala 1977, 1996

One Dharma: The Emerging Western Buddhism
  Joseph Goldstein. Published by Harper San Francisco 2002

Psychoanalysis and Buddhism: An Unfolding Dialogue
  Edited by Jeremy D. Safran. Published by Wisdom Publications 2003

Radiant Mind: Essential Buddhist Teachings
  Edited by Jean Smith. Published by Riverhead Books
  The Berkeley Publishing Group 1999 ❖

Toward a Psychology of Awakening
  John Welwood, Ph.D. Published by Shambhala 2000, 2002

Women's Buddhism, Buddhism's Women
  Edited by Ellison Banks Findly. Published by Wisdom
  Publications 2000

Zen and the Brain
  James H. Austin, M.D.. Published by MIT Press 1998, 1999

Zen Training: Methods and Philosophy
  Katsuki Sekida. Published by Shambhala Classics
  1985, 2005

Christianity

Christian Mystics: Their Lives and Legacies
  Ursula King. Published by Hidden Spring 1985, 2001

The Experience of No-Self: A Contemplative Journey
  Bernadette Roberts. Published by Shambhala 1982, 1993

The Flowering of Mysticism: Men and Women in the New Mysticism: 1200-1350
  Bernard McGinn. Published by Crossroad Publishing 1998

The Foundations of Mysticism: Origins to the Fifth Century
  Bernard McGinn. Published by Crossroad Publishing
  1991, 2004

The Growth of Mysticism: Gregory the Great through the 12th Century
  Bernard McGinn. Published by Crossroad Publishing
  1994, 1999

The Luminous Vision: Six Medieval Mystics and their Teachings
  Anne Bancroft. Published by Unwin Paperbacks 1982, 1989

Mystics of the Christian Tradition
  Steven Fanning. Published by Routledge 2001 ❖

New Seeds of Contemplation
  Thomas Merton. Published by New Directions 1961, 2007

Orthodox Spirituality
  Father Lev Gillet, a Monk of the Eastern Church. Published by St. Vladimir Seminary Press 1945, 1987 ❖

The Roots of Christian Mysticism
  Olivier Clement. Published by New City Press 1982, 1995 ❖

Silence and Witness: The Quaker Tradition
  Michael L. Birkel. Published by Orbis Books 2004

Hinduism

Daughters of the Goddess: Women Saints of India
  Linda Johnsen. Published by Yes International 1994 ❖

The Deeper Dimensions of Yoga: Theory and Practice
  Georg Feuerstein. Published by Shambhala 2003

The Essential Swami Ramdas
  Compiled with intro. by Susunaga Weeraperuma. Published by World Wisdom 2005

Hinduism: Its Meaning for the Liberation of the Spirit
  Swami Nikhilananda. Published by Ramakrishna-Vivekananda Center 1958, 1992 ❖

I Have Become Alive: Secrets of the Inner Journey
  Swami Muktananda. Published by SYDA Foundation 1985, 1992

The Life Divine
  Sri Aurobindo. Published by E.P. Dutton & Co. 1949, 2006 ❖

Light on Life: The Yoga Journey to Wholeness, Inner Peace, and Ultimate Freedom
  B.K.S. Iyengar. Published by Rodale Inc. 2005

The Spiritual Teaching of Ramana Maharshi
  Forward by Carl Jung. Published by Shambhala 1972, 2004 ❖

Sri Ramakrishna: Prophet for a New Age
  Richard Schiffman. Published by Paragon House 1989

Vivekananda: Lessons in Classical Yoga
  Edited by Dave DeLuca. Published by Namaste Books 2003

Yoga & Psychotherapy: Evolution of Consciousness
  Rama, Ballentine, Ajaya. Published by Himalayan International Institute 1978, 1981

Islam

Awakening: A Sufi Experience
  Pir Vilayat Inayat Khan. Published by Jeremy P. Tarcher/Putnam 1999, 2000 ❖

Essential Sufism
  Edited by James Fadiman & Robert Franger. Published by HarpersSan Francisco 1985, 1999

The Garden of Truth: The Vision and Promise of Sufism
  Seyyed Hossein Nasr. Published by HarperCollins 2007

The Knowing Heart: A Sufi Path of Transformation
  Kabir Helminski. Published by Shambhala 1972, 2004

Mystical Dimensions of Islam
  Annemarie Schimmel. Published by University of North Carolina Press 1975, 1978 ❖

The Mystics of Islam
  Reynold A. Nicholson. Published by World Wisdom Inc. 1914, 2002

The Shambhala Guide to Sufism
  Carl W. Ernst. Published by Shambhala 1997

Sufi Essays
  Seyyed Hossein Nasr. Published by State University of New York Press 1972, 1999

Sufism: Love & Wisdom
  Edited by Jean-Louis Michon & Roger Gaetani. Published by World Wisdom 2006

The Way of the Sufi
  Idries Shah. Published by E.P. Dutton & Co. 1970, 1990 ❖

Women of Sufism: A Hidden Treasure
  Camille Adams Helminski. Published by Shambhala 2003

Judaism

The Essential Kabbalah: Heart of Jewish Mysticism
  Daniel C. Matt. Published by Castle Books 1995, 1997 ❖

God is a Verb: Kabbalah and Practice of Mystical Judaism
  David A. Cooper. Published by Riverhead Books 1997, 1998

I and Thou
  Martin Buber. Published by Simon & Schuster 1937, 2006

Jewish Mystical Testimonies
  Compiled by Louis Jacobs. Published by Schoken Books 1976, 1997

Kabbalah: The Mystic Quest in Judaism
  David S. Ariel. Published by Jason Aronson 1988, 2006

Kabbalah: New Perspectives
  Mose Idel. Published by Yale University Press 1988, 1990 ❖

Kabbalah: The Way of the Jewish Mystic
  Perle Epstein. Published by Shambhala Classics 1978, 2001 ❖

Major Trends in Jewish Mysticism
  Gershom Scholem. Published by Schoken Books 1946, 1995

Meditation and Kabbalah
  Aryeh Kaplan. Published by Weiser Books 1982, 1994

Sacred Therapy: Jewish Spiritual Teachings
  Estelle Frankel. Published by Shambhala 2003, 2005

The Work of the Kabbalist
  Z'ev ben Shimon Halevi [Warren Kenton]. Published by Weiser Books 1985, 1993

Comparative Studies

Between Jersusalem and Benares
  Edited by Hananya Goodman. Published by State University of New York Press 1994 (J/H)

Christian & Islamic Spirituality: Sharing a Journey
  Maria Jaoudi. Published by Paulist Press 1985, 1993 (C/I)

The Gospel of John in the Light of Indian Mysticism
  Ravi Ravindra. Published by Inner Traditions 1990, 2004
  (C/H)

A Meeting of Mystic Paths: Christianity and Yoga
  Justin O'Brien. Published by Yes International 1996 (C/H)

The One Light: Bede Griffith's Principal Writings
  Edited by Bruno Barnhart. Published by Templegate
  Publishers 2001 (C/H)

Paths to the Heart: Sufism and the Christian East
  Edited by James S. Cutsinger. Published by World Wisdom,
  Inc. 2002, 2004 (I/C)

Philosophies of India
  Heinrich Zimmer. Published by Princeton University Press
  1951, 2008 (H/ J/ B)

The Soul of the Story: Meetings with Remarkable People
  Rabbi David Zeller. Published by Jewish Lights Publishing
  2006 (J/H)

Speaking of Silence: Christians and Buddhists on the Contemplative Way
  Susan Walker. Published by Paulist Press 1987

Three Ways of Asian Wisdom
  Nancy Wilson Ross. Published by Simon and Schuster
  1966, 1996 (H/B)

Mysticism

The Enlightened Mind: An anthology of sacred prose
  Edited by Stephen Mitchell. Published by HarperPerennial/
  HarperCollins 1991, 1993 ❖

The Essential Mystics: The Soul's Journey into Truth
  Andrew Harvey. Published by Castle Books 1996, 1998 ❖

For the Love of God: Handbook for the Spirit
  Edited by R. Carlson & B. Shield. Published by New World Library 1990, 2008

God In All Worlds: An Anthology of Contemporary Spiritual Writing
  Edited by Lucinda Vardey. Published by Pantheon Books 1995

Graceful Exists: How Great Beings Die
  Edited by Sushila Blackman. Published by Shambhala 1997, 2005

Halfway Up The Mountain: The Error of Premature Claims to Enlightment
  M. Caplan. Published by Hohm Press 2001

History of Mysticism: The Unchanging Testament
  S. Abhayananda [Stan Trout]. Published by Atma Books ❖ 1987, 1996

An Idealist View of Life
  Sarvepalli Radhakrishnan. Published by George Allen & Unwin Ltd. 1932, 2003 ❖

Living Deeply: The Art and Science of Transformation in Everyday Life
  M. Schiltz, C. Vieten, T. Amorok. Published by New Harbinger Publications 2007

The Mystic Heart: Discovering a Universal Spirituality in the World's Religions
  Wayne Teasdale. Published by New World Library 1999, 2001

PRIMARY BIBLIOGRAPHY

The Mystical Mind: Probing the Biology of Religious Experience
  Newberg, D'Aquili. Published by Fortress Press 1999

Mysticism: A Study in Nature and Development of Spiritual Consciousness
  Evelyn Underhill. Published currently by KDP 1911, 2011 ❖

Mysticism: Holiness East and West
  Denise and John Carmody. Published by Oxford University Press 1996

Mysticism, Mind, Consciousness
  Robert K.C. Forman. Published by State University of New York Press 1999

Mysticism of Now: The Art of Being Alive
  Rafael Catala. Published by Acropolis Books 1998

Mysticism: A Study and Anthology
  F.C. Happold. Published by Penguin Books 1963, 1990

Mysticism in the World's Religion
  Geoffrey Parrinder. Published by Oneworld Publications 1976, 1996 ❖

Mysticism in World Religions
  Sidney Spencer. Published by Penguin Books 1963, 1971 ❖

Mystics, Masters, Saints, and Sages
  R. Ullman, J. Reichenber-Ullman. Published by Conari Press 2001

One Cosmos under God: The Unification of Matter, Life, Mind and Spirit
  by Robert W. Godwin. Published by Paragon House 2004

One River, Many Wells: Wisdom Springing from Global Faiths
   Matthew Fox. Published by Jeremy Thatcher/Penguin 2000, 2004

The Perennial Philosophy
   Aldous Huxley. Published by Perennial division of HarperCollins 1944, 2004 ❖

Quantum Questions: Mystical Writings of the World's Great Physicists
   Edited by Ken Wilber. Published by Shambhala 1984, 2001

Quantum Theology: Spiritual Implications of the New Physics
   Diarmuid O'Murchu. Published by Crossroad Publishing 2004

Secret Splendor: The Journey Within
   Charles Earnest Essert. Published by Mystics of the World 1973, 2019

The Simple Feeling of Being: Embracing Your True Nature
   Ken Wilber. Published by Shambhala 2004

The Spiritual Athlete: A Primer for the Inner Life
   Compiled and edited by Ray Berry. Published by Joshua Press 1992, 2000

The Spiritual Brain: A Neuroscientist's Case for the Existence of the Soul
   M. Beauregard, D. O'Leary. Published by HarperCollins 2007

Spiritual Evolution: Scientists Discuss Their Beliefs
   Edited by John Marks Templeton. Published by Templeton Foundation Press 1998

Surprised by Grace: A Journey Beyond Personal Enlightenment
  Amber Terrell. Published by True Light Publishing 1997, 2003

The Transcendent Unity of Religions
  Frithjof Schuon. Published by A Quest Book 1984, 1993

Transcending the Levels of Consciousness
  David R. Hawkins, M.D., Ph.D.. Published by Veritas Publishing 2006

A Treasury of Traditional Wisdom: An Encyclopedia of Humankind's Spiritual Truth
  Whitall N. Perry. Published by Fons Vitae 1971, 2000

The Visionary Window: A Quantum Physicist's Guide to Enlightenment
  A. Goswami. Published by Quest Books 2000, 2006

Why God Won't Go Away: Brain Science & the Biology of Belief
  A. Newberg, E. D'Aquili. Published by Ballantine 2001

Other References

Autism and the God Connection
  William Stillman. Published by Sourcebooks Inc. 2006

The Concise Guide to World Religions
  Eliade, Couliano. Published by HarperCollins San Francisco 1991, 2000 ❖

Dictionary of Philosophy and Religion: Eastern & Western Thought
  W. Reese. Published by Humanity Books 1980, 1999 ❖

Dictionary of Psychology
  Edited by Arthur S. Reber & Emily S. Reber. Published by Penguin Books 1985, 2001 ❖

God: A Brief History: The Human Search for Eternal Truth
  John Bowker. Published by DK Publishing 2002

God in the Equation: How Einstein Transformed Religion
  Corey S. Powell. Published by Free Press / Simon and Schuster 2002, 2005

A History of God: The 4, 000-Year Quest of Judaism, Christianity and Islam
  Karen Armstrong. Published by Gramercy Books 1993, 2004

Life after Death in World Religions
  Edited by Harold Coward. Published by Orbis Books 1997

The New Penguin Handbook of Living Religions
  Edited by John R. Hinnells. Published by Penguin Books 1997, 2003 ❖

Oxford Dictionary of World Religions
  Edited by John Bowker. Published by Oxford University Press 1997, 2005 ❖

The Religion Book: Encyclopedia of Places, Prophets, Saints, & Seers
  J. Willis. Published by Visible Ink 2004

World Religions: From Ancient History to the Present
  Edited by Geoffrey Parrinder. Published by Facts on File Inc. 1971, 1985 ❖

Wikipedia
  The Internet encyclopedia [data on the Universe, Earth, the human species, and the history of each].

MYSTICAL APPROACHES TO LIFE

The Big Picture

WHAT IF YOU went to a theater to watch a movie* and, instead of sitting in their seats, you brought your own chair and sat directly in front of the screen? You might block the projector and cast your own shadow; you surely would not see the entire picture. It sounds foolish, yet that is the way many people view this life: separate and too close. Cinerama is useless when looked at with *my*opic eyes.

We often bring our own baggage to this life's experiences and are so concerned with how we appear that we cannot clearly observe what is directly in front of us, nor what is happening all around us. Some call this tunnel vision; mystics call it ignorance. When you gaze at life with dark glasses of your self, through lenses that are clouded with your ego and individuality, you confuse the apparent with the real. You must remove those glasses to see this life as it is.

We are so close to our subjective impressions that we frequently imagine them to be reality. We must stand back and look at the big picture to understand things as they truly relate to one another, not solely as they relate to "me." Most people have doors between "me"

---

* To appreciate "Life," the movie, be aware of the divine theater in which it is playing.

and "them." Some open them wide so that others are welcome in, many crack them barely enough so they can step out briefly, while a few keep their doors shut and just peek at life through a peep hole.

Psychiatrists have terms for these personality types, yet we might notice them daily ... except, perhaps, our own. We each erect many emotional, mental and/or physical barriers to help protect us from unwanted guests. Some mystics say that you should not only keep those doors open, you should remove them from their hinges and throw them away! The divine essence is just outside your door, but when you keep it closed it cannot come in to transform your life.

"Wait a minute! Mystics say that the divine is already in my soul." True, but where is *your* soul? It is not isolated in that little room you call your self; it is not subsisting on feeding your ego and drunk with your individuality. It is the divine essence waiting outside your own barriers, present presently in this place at this moment. Clean up the mess you made with *I, me* and *my* and let it in. It is not your soul until you allow it to join your self as an honored guest in your home.

When you observe the big picture you can see this life as it is here and now, not only with respect to your past or how it could possibly influence your future. There are, of course, wider screens for you to consider. Will what is happening here affect those you love? Might it impact the people of your community or nation? Can it bring you and them closer to the divine? A disturbance in the ocean now can cause waves crashing on distant shores. Here and now is important.

Stare into an observatory telescope; you can then glimpse the immensity of this Universe. Peer through an electron microscope; you will marvel at the miracle of life. Simply seeing without any aids can be quite deceptive. The sun seems to rise in the East and set in the West, prior to studying astronomy. Earth looks flat, without the lessons of geography. Lightning appears close, until you later hear thunder. In darkness, a rope could be confused with a snake.

Superficial judgments are often in error. Our emotions, mind and senses can be fooled. We build beliefs based on past experiences or what we have been taught, but what if they were mistaken? Mystics say that you must go beyond the pleasures and disappointments of this life's loves to realize divine Love. It is also necessary to surpass the little truths of today to accept eternal divine Truth. Transcend everyday realities to be aware of divine Reality. Live in the divine.

Have you used the zoom lens on a camera? You can change the focus from a wide angle perspective, with limited detail, to a narrow view with its images enlarged. Unfortunately, that is a compromise we must make with most of our experiences in this life. When we do consider the overall aspect of here and now, we better understand how it can effect all of life. We might, then, overlook some critical details. When we zoom in on the specifics of what is happening, we might not appreciate their greater implications. "Catch-22."

True mystics, however, say that you can do both. By opening up to that divine flow of endless Love, absolute Truth and ultimate Reality, from the widest outlook, we can then better understand many of the specifics of the more focused views required in daily living. Mortal loves become richer, mundane truths will make more sense, and worldly realities of today are seen in the wider setting of the divine. It will alter the way the ambiguities of this life affect you.

From a divine perspective, in the context of eternity, there will be less anxiety, fewer worries and reduced pain from this transient life's troubles. In the universal background of infinity, however, our prestige, self-importance and achievements will have diminished significance. We attain equanimity which prevents wild fluctuations. Our horizons expand. Living becomes greater. The big picture will make this life seem smaller. Here and now surpass space and time.

Our Different Worlds

EVERY PERSON LIVES in different worlds at various phases of their life. Our feelings, conceptions and perceptions may vary in each of those worlds. Parents look at many situations unlike their children; a reversal of their own much earlier experiences. In youth we saw things from simpler points of view than we do in our later years. Our level of awareness, tastes, needs, and desires evolve as we progress through stages of our lives. In mundane living, priorities are not constant.

Within each stage of life, people move between diverse worlds. Our roles and behavior at home and among family might deviate greatly from those at work and with our associates. Our position as an expert or, at least, an experienced person in certain aspects of life may be reversed in other areas. Hobbies and other personal interests bring people into enjoyable worlds outside work requirements and family obligations. Also, shifting moods and concerns, ours and others', can modify the same worlds from day to day. Situations do change, like it or not.

Our worlds can also be affected by fluctuating states of our being. When we are emotionally balanced our vision of life is better than during, or after, traumatic experiences. A person with a sound mind may become delusional during mental illness; even our imagination can take us into different worlds. When our bodies are healthy our outlook is usually brighter than during a sickness or after an injury. A handicapped person may approach our worlds from perspectives altered, often outside of their control, from those of people with no such disability. The physical world itself alters from day to day.

Buddhism teaches that there is no continuing self, just the fleeting *skandhas*. To some extent, psychologists and physiologists would agree. Skandhas are the five aggregates of all human beings: bodily matter; sensations; perceptions; mental formations; consciousness. "They are constantly in the process of change and do not constitute a self." Psychologists say that our mind is always in a state of flux and the make-up of our psyche varies each moment. Physiologists attest to the ever altering state of our body: cells are dying and then regenerated continuously, following DNA patterns which make the modifications appear to be gradual. Trauma can speed the process.

Christians, Hindus, Jews, and Muslims — as well as most Buddhists in daily life — accept continuity of self, while acknowledging changes in the emotions, mind and body of each person. Also, to a greater or lesser degree, they do accept presence of a soul in each human. They do not all agree, however, that the soul has the essence of the divine, as most mystics believe. Most people live in their immediate emotional, mental and physical self, or skandhas, but some include various levels of spirituality to make life more meaningful for them.

Those people who believe in the soul* usually also believe that it provides the vital or spiritual energy needed to make all aspects of our self function. The more prominent is our soul, in theory, then the better person we will be. The soul, however, is elusive; it cannot be specifically identified. Mystics intuitively *know* we can transcend our self to live through the soul, reunited with the essence of the divine. This is the wonderful world of divine union in this life.

Our worldview depends, then, on our perspective. The material world may be the same, but our discernment of it can transform its meanings. Some people approach many activities and events from outlooks beyond their self. Their personal world may include their social group, community, nation, or, rarely, all humankind. A few can see beyond the impact on humanity; they might consider the world of all living beings and, perhaps, all of Nature itself. Mystics approach life from the perspective of the divine: as the divine does.

The world of mystics is broader in scope than of those who have not reunited with their soul. True mystics are able to see oneness in All: everything is interrelated, existing at the spaceless here, in the timeless now. They deny accepted limits of experiencing the world and the boundaries of *this* life. Their worldview has expanded to a universal vista, in a divine panorama, into a focus from wholeness embracing all emotional, mental, physical, *and* spiritual aspects of every activity and event beyond any specific feelings, conceptions or perceptions. Each

---

* In Buddhism "self/soul" are false beliefs, mental projections; "anatman" is no self/soul.

person is capable of this all-encompassing vision, but must first be dedicated to realizing it. It might happen suddenly.

In apparent realities, we all seem to live in different personal worlds, while within the same material world. In true Reality our worlds are always One: interpenetrating, inseparable and divine.

> Note: Historical and cultural worlds must be considered; our society today is more secular than in other eras of our nation or is currently in some other countries.

Quotations of Mystics

Mysticism in World Religion
  Sidney Spencer. Published by Penguin Books 1963, 1971

"At the goal, the soul is filled with and enveloped in the love of God. It is indistinguishable from God ... all thought of lover, love and the beloved is absent."
Swami S(h)ivananda (H)

[Nirvana is] "the annihilation of the ego-conception, freedom from subjectivity, insight into the essence of Suchness, the recognition of the oneness of existence."
Ashvaghosha (B)

"Do not err in this matter of self and other. Everything is Buddha without exception. Here is that immaculate and final stage, where thought is pure in its true nature."
Saraha (B)

Note: (b. 769) Bengali mendicant celebrated for his songs on realization.

"The man who has felt the divine touch and perceived its nature is no longer separated from his Master, and behold, he is his Master, and his Master is he, for he is so intimately united to Him that he cannot by any means be separated from Him." Abulafia (J)

"Everything is in Thee and Thou art everything; Thou fillest everything and Thou dost encompass it."
Eleazar of Worms (J)

"The universe is the outward visible expression of the Real, and the Real is the inner unseen Reality of the universe."
Jami (I)

"The heart [soul] has two doors, the one turned towards outer things, the other towards the inner kingdom — this door is that of inspiration and revelation." al-Ghazali (I)

"Suddenly God came and united Himself to me in a manner quite ineffable. Without any 'confusion of persons' He entered into every part of my being, as fire penetrates iron, or light streams through glass."
St. Simeon [Symeon the New Theologian] (C)

"He has created each person's soul as a living mirror, on which he has impressed the image of his nature. In this way he lives imaged forth in us and we in him, for our created life is one ... with this image and life which we have eternally in God." Ruysbroek (C)

The Essential Mystics
Andrew Harvey. Published by Castle Books 1996, 1998

"Truth is one; It is called by different names [from the Rig Veda]. From a lake ... the Hindus take water in jars and call it 'jal' ... Muslims take water in leather bags and call it 'pani' ... the Christians take the same thing and call it 'water.' Suppose someone says that the thing is not jal but pani, or that it is not pani but water, or that it is not water but jal. It would indeed be ridiculous." Ramakrishna (H)

Note: He realized divine union within each of all three faiths.

"Every grain of matter, every appearance is one with Eternal and Immutable Reality! Wherever your foot may fall, you are still within the Sanctuary for Enlightenment, though it is nothing perceptible." Huang-po (B)

"*Each molecule teaches perfect law, each moment chants true sutra.*" Shutaku (1308–1388) (B)

"*God is unified oneness—one without two; inestimable. Genuine divine existence engenders the existence of all creation. The sublime, inner essences secretly constitute a chain linking everything from the highest to the lowest to the edge of the universe.*" Moses de Leon (J)

"*There is one who sings the song of his soul, discovering in his soul everything: utter spiritual fulfillment. Then there is one who expands even further until he unites with all existence, with all creatures, with all worlds, singing a song with all of them.*" Abraham Isaac Kook (J)

"*You thought yourself part, small; whereas in you is a universe, the greatest.*" Hazreti 'Ali (I)

Note: (599–661) Son–in–law of the Prophet Muhammed.

"*Listen with faith to the call 'In all truth, I am God.' He who knows Reality, to whom Unicity is revealed, sees at first gaze the Light of Being. He perceives by illumination that pure light. He sees God first in everything he sees.*" Shabestari (I)

Note: (1250-1320) Persian Sufi

"*When I turn back beyond my senses and reason and pass through the door into eternal life, I discover my true Self [soul], then I begin to see the world as it really is.*" Bede Griffiths (C)

Note: Quotations relate to the summary as a whole, rather than to any one essay.

A Divine Formula?

THERE CANNOT BE a *divine formula*, not even a *you formula*. This is just one suggestion for understanding relationships between spirit, matter and mind, apart from most of the traditions of mysticism.

Some theologians, philosophers and mystics proposed theories of cosmology, cosmogony or cosmography: the order or underlying structure of this Universe, its creation and its description or extent. Few of them offered a mathematical formula in their explanations.

Albert Einstein revolutionized physics in 1905 with his Special Theory of Relativity. His formula, $E=mc^2$, states that energy equals mass at the speed of light squared. The speed of all light is 186,262 miles per *second*. That means all particles of matter, e.g. atoms, contain vast potential energy, e.g. one gram can produce 25 million kWh of electricity: the foundation for developing nuclear power.

Perhaps we can reinterpret, and adjust, that formula to help clarify the correlation between divine Essence, matter and consciousness: $E=mc^{f(x)}$. Unlike the speed of light, which is a constant, there are now no exact measurements for consciousness. In this hypothetical formula, basic consciousness may be of insects, to the second power of animals and to the third power the rational mind of humans. The fourth power is suprarational consciousness of mystics, when they intuit the divine essence in *perceived* matter.

Divine essence might be felt as spiritual energy, an interpretation acceptable to many religions and mystics. Matter is the mass, the apparent physical makeup of this Universe. As spiritual awareness, suprarational consciousness could figuratively be "seeing the light" or, more literally, penetrating the cloud of ignorance that prevents people from realizing the divine. Some mystics speak of awareness of a divine light; Einstein himself said that the *"most beautiful and profound emotion we can experience is the sensation of the mystical."*

Einstein's Special Theory has the surprising consequences that "the same event, when viewed from inertial systems in motion with respect to each other, will seem to occur at different times, bodies will measure out at different lengths, and clocks will run at different speeds." Light does travel in a curve, due to the gravity of matter, thereby distorting views from each perspective in this Universe.

Similarly, mystics' consciousness in divine oneness, viewed from various historical, cultural and personal perspectives, have occurred with different frequencies, degrees of realization and durations. This might help to explain the diversity in the expressions or reports of that spiritual awareness. What is seen is the same; it is the *seeing* which differs.

In some sciences, all existence is described as matter or energy. In some of mysticism, only consciousness exists. Dark matter is 25%, and dark energy about 70%, of the critical density of this Universe.* Divine essence (grace, love, spirit), also not visible, emanates and sustains universal matter (mass/energy: visible/dark) and cosmic consciousness ($cf(x)$ raised to its greatest power). During suprarational consciousness, *and beyond*, mystics share in that essence to varying extents.

The Special Theory of Relativity might be called "the outer way," examining this Universe as a whole to ascertain the relationships between energy and mass. An atom is a microcosm of the Universe. Conversely, nuclear physics could be described as the "inner way," exploring the atom, or mass, to discover means to tap the power, or energy, potentially within it. Dual approaches to the same force.

Most traditions of mysticism, and most mystics, recommended the inner way: exploring a person's inner self, or soul, to discover the divine essence inherent in it. The speculative divine formula might be said to be the outer way, to examine all matter to ascertain the spiritual quintessence which eternally unifies all existence. This examination is not sensory nor subject to accurate measurement.

The so-called "Nature mystics," who might be either religious or non-religious, may have felt the spiritual essence of birds, of trees, of rivers, and of mountains. Many faiths other than the five major religions worship spirits of the sky, of earth, of animals, and of their ancestors. They all do, of course, experience their surroundings

---

* These widely accepted theories imply that science can now study only 5% of this Universe. For an excellent article search for "NASA Dark Energy, Dark Matter" on the Internet.

by sight, sound, smell, touch, and/or taste, but also, more significantly, by using a figurative "sixth sense," which is defined as intuition.

Intuition plays an important role in the mysticism of all religions; it gives an insight into the divine essence. Intuitive insight, looking without or within, is just a prelude to divine union. Looking without, expanded consciousness of matter allows us to realize its spiritual quintessence and ours. Looking within, greater consciousness of our own divine essence enables us to realize it in all matter. These are two approaches to one goal: experiencing divine Reality.

Divine Truth is joined by divine Love and grace when we give our own love to all on Earth, in this Universe and beyond. For many mystics, divine Love *is* the unitive essence ... the energy of the soul.

Upside Down

AN "UPSIDE" OF THIS life might be a "downside" for mysticism. Some ideals that many people were taught are to be independent, to gain self-confidence and be self-sufficient. Yet, the very independence of our individuality, augmented with assuredness and autonomy, can minimize our interdependence on one another and may lead us away from both full spirituality and consciousness in divine union. It can build our egos into blinders, closing out the true Reality.

We might recognize the blinders of *other* people. Some persons seem to move through this life unaware of many matters which we believe to be important. Our list might include material concerns, ethical and moral considerations, sensitivity to their surroundings, and/or care for the well-being of ourselves and others. However, we are too seldom aware of our own blinders, or we are unwilling to rectify all of our already acknowledged shortcomings.

Many people prefer to "go with the flow," finding conformity much easier than looking into their inner self. The need to "fit in," to be accepted by others and to not "cause waves" could diminish their individuality. Unfortunately, there are those who have a poor self-image and are debilitated by self-doubt, insecurity, and racked by guilt, real or imagined. They may be said to create their own *hell*.

Mysticism seeks to remove the blinders of this life, to expand our horizons beyond usual and accepted norms, to surpass restrictions of conditioned sentiments, ideas and sensations. Diffusion of the One into the many, which the Kabbalah calls the "breaking of the vessels," is a cause for the sufferings of humans which the Buddha strove to overcome. Attachment to the fictions of this life, which Hindus call *maya*, prevents the compassion and mercy of the divine, sought by Muslims, from entering our lives. Seeking to satisfy our superficial ego ignores the "kingdom of God" within us which Jesus urged us to discover. Each of us create the barriers to our own spiritual realization.

There seems to be a paradox to mystics' vision. On the one hand, they say that we must find our own inner self, or soul, a true self-realization which discovers the divinity inherent within us. On the other hand, they also say that all souls are One, that there is unity to all existence beyond multiple and individual manifestations. This paradox exists only in rational consciousness, which tries to explain everything with reason, logic or images. That limits our experience.

Suprarational consciousness, complete intuitive insight realized in divine grace, is aware that our soul and all other souls are divine *and* that the spirits of the many are united in the Spirit of the One, *without contradiction*. Certainty of oneness overcomes most of the uncertainties of this life; liberation from ego and individuality leads to a freedom seldom experienced in worldly existence. Many of the downsides of ordinary living become upsides during divine living.

In this life, most people move much like a small boat in an ocean, rolling up on a wave of happiness, then sinking down with sadness, punctuated with pleasant calm seas and the occasional turbulent storm. Confusing feelings too often reign in the individual, ego self.

Opening up our self, which is an act of courage or faith, allows the divine Love, Truth and Reality to enter. We typically close them out in a desperate attempt to hold on to our sense of uniqueness. Divine Love is constant and never ending, unlike ups and downs of loves in daily lives. Divine Truth does not change as some apparent truths in this life do. Divine Reality is eternal; too many mundane realities seem to be replaced just as we grow accustomed to them.

Faith is entering an intersection of life on a green light, expecting that the crossing traffic will stop. Belief is after looking both ways before proceeding, sure that no one will hit you. By your studying of mysticism, learning from teachings of sages throughout the ages, you can gain faith in the possibility of divine union. By looking deep into your inner self, toward the divine in *your* soul, you may attain a belief in oneness with the divine which can spur you onwards.

Approaching the divine is often said to be similar to ascending a mountain or to descending into an ocean. In divine unity, there is no up or down, no metaphorical mountain or ocean, there simply *is*. Anyone who describes paradise is speaking from memories of their schooling or is trying to paint pictures so listeners can understand. They might mention a bright light, but that is less an incandescence than an illumination which removes the darkness of ignorance.

Throughout this life we try to gratify our personal cravings. We might desire comforts and pleasures, recognition and respect, and/or wealth and possessions. Pursuit of mortal satisfactions leave little time for seeking the divine. Most mystics say that even praying to see God or asking for entry into heaven are misguided. We must completely surrender ourself, our separate self, to the divine will; in a paraphrase, it is to "go with the *universal* flow."

> Note: Here, "faith" is what is taught to be correct; "belief" is what is personally felt to be true. In their usage, correctly defined, each word may mean the reverse.

Looking Beyond

THE DIVINE IS in you; you are not as yet in the divine. The greatest achievement in life is living in the infinite and eternal within us. Seeking the absolute and ultimate—the mystical quest—is a part of everyone's life, still we seldom consciously and actively participate in it. You must truly believe in divine oneness and the possibility of reuniting in this life. Belief alone will not bring divine union, but too much doubt will probably ensure not being fully awakened to it.

You might also want to read some of the books quoted before deciding on the mystical journey. You are cautioned, however, that no words on any number of pages can ever completely explain that quest. Reading will raise more questions and the answers are not to be found in any books. Poems, parables, narratives, and analogies can only give you clues. Learning about other people's experiences may provide glimpses, yet never replace direct experience.

You must seek to realize a perspective on all of existence beyond all of your own prior experiences or knowledge: unlike any of those sentiments that you have felt, any thoughts that you have conceived or any sensations that you have perceived in this life, using a direct mode of *knowing*. Here are a few imperfect analogies to assist in better understanding the challenges which you might encounter:

Imagine that you are a drop of blood within your body. As you move through its blood vessels, you become aware of the passing presence of organs, bones and tissue, yet believe this body to be the only reality there is or, at least, which can be known. Unexpectedly, there is a puncture in the skin just as you approach and you spurt forth in search of other realities. Outside, you discover a world which surpasses any that you had previously experienced. You may have been pumped out for testing, for transfusion into another body, or be washed away to be absorbed in this much wider existence. You will certainly be tested; you might even be born again; washing away your *self* can result in reunion with the divine.

It would be easier for an artist to paint a symphony, or for a composer to orchestrate a painting, than for any mystic to describe what it is like to be in divine oneness. At least both art and music can somewhat highlight each other. Mystics are so aware of the limits of human forms of expression that most do not even attempt to portray what they experienced with all of their being and which has transformed their lives. To them, skeptics do not matter. They may only assist those who want to realize union with the ground of existence.

Spiritual *knowing*, mystical gnosis,* is *complete intuitive insight*. It combines the very definition of all three words. *Complete*: "The entirety needed for realization; consummate." *Intuitive*: "Knowing something without rational processes; the immediate cognition of it." *Insight*:

---

* "Gnosis" (Greek) is somewhat equivalent to "da`at" (Hebrew), "jnana" (Sanskrit), "ma`rifa" (Arabic), or "panna" (Pali), each as a means of spiritual knowing.

"Discernment of the true nature of a situation; the penetration beyond the reach of the senses." Complete intuitive insight precedes divine unity and usually follows it. It is suprarational. Union with the divine, however, surpasses knower, known and knowing; it is to be at one with the divine essence. It is not to be the divine, but to be in the divine as the divine is. It is sharing in universal consciousness.

Books on mysticism may speak of transcendence and immanence. *Transcendence*: "Passing beyond human limit; independent of any material experience." *Immanence*: "Existing or remaining within; inherent." Unity with the divine is both. You must go beyond your *self* to be in the divine. To be in the soul, the divine in you, is to be in the divine. The divine is not just in you, it is in All: animate and inanimate; on Earth and in this entire Universe; emotional, mental, physical, and spiritual; anything, everything, but yet no *thing*.

Few people, of any age or state of health, want to even consider their own death. All of us, however, realize that death is inevitable. Consider its definitions: death is only the end of this life and the demise of this body. Unless you believe it is *The End*, death is also the threshold of a new beginning. How many possibilities follow this life? Few people have been so good that they have earned eternal paradise; fewer want to go to a place where they must receive punishments for their sins. Those who do believe in resurrection of their body hope that it will be not be in its final form. Few people really want to continue to be born again and live more human lives; fewer want to be reborn in a non-human form. If you are not quite certain you want to seek divine oneness, consider the alternatives.

This short life is just a speck in time; it is important to us because it now seems to be our speck. Look beyond yesterday, today and tomorrow, beyond Earth's 4.5 billion years: consider eternity.

> Note: In the Kabbalah of Judaism, the infinite "Ein Sof" emanates "Shekhinah," the immanent divine presence. To be infinite is to be both immanent and transcendent.

Quotations of Mystics

History of Mysticism
S. Abhayananda [Stan Trout] Published by Atma Books
1987, 1996

"He who is escaping from God flees to himself; he who escapes from his own mind flees to the Mind of the universe, confessing that all things of the human mind are vain and unreal, and attributing everything to God." Philo (J)

"May I be far removed from contending creeds and dogmas. Ever since my Lord's grace entered my mind, My mind has never strayed to seek such distractions." Milarepa (B)

"When the mystery of the oneness of the soul and the Divine is revealed to you, you will understand that you are no other than God." Ibn (al-) Arabi (I)

"Because He is Himself the absolute Ground, in which all contrariety is unity, all diversity is identity, that which we understand as diversity cannot exist in God."
Nicholas of Cusa (C)

"One cannot see God without His grace. ... to receive the grace of God one must renounce egotism; one cannot see God as long as one feels "I am the doer."
Ramakrishna (H)

Mystical Dimensions of Islam
Annemarie Schimmel. Published by Univ. of North Carolina Press 1975, 1976 (I)

"The gnostics [true mystics] ... are drawing nearer to God. They are not themselves, but in so far as they exist at all they exist in God. Their movements are caused by God

... *their words are the words of God ... their sight is the sight of God.*" Dhu'l-Nun al-Misri

[fana] "I was brought toward complete annihilation and gratified by ending individuality and outward traces, and was exalted to 'remaining in God'; and after the ascent I was sent toward the descent, and the door of Divine Law was opened to me." Khwaja Mir Dard

Note: (1721–85) Naqshbandi Sufi in Delhi; went from intoxication and exuberance to a sober (gnostic) attitude.

Kabbalah — New Perspectives
Moshe Idel. Published by Yale University Press
1988, 1990 (J)

[devekut / cleaving] " ... causes him to pass from potentiality into the final and perfect actuality, and he and He become one entity, inseparable during this act." Abraham Abulafia

"This is true cleaving, as he becomes one substance with God into whom he was swallowed, without being separate to be considered as a distinct entity."
Shne'ur Zalman of Lyady

Daughters of the Goddess: Women Saints of India
Linda Johnsen. Published by Yes International 1994 (H)

"Meditate on the divinity within yourself. Drink the nectar of love that continually pours from the heart of God." Lalla

Note: She was the 14th century prophetess of Kashmir.

"Spiritual love is different. ... it leads to unity with the beloved. This unity in love remains forever and ever, always alive, both within and without, and each moment you live in love. It will swallow you completely until there is no 'you.' There is only love." Amritanandamayi Ma [Amma(chi)]

Note: (1953–) 20th–21st century saint; she is called the "hugging saint."

Mystics of the Christian Tradition
Steven Fanning. Published by Routledge 2001 (C)

[the unitive way] *"At the very onset of [mystical] prayer the mind is taken hold of by the divine and infinite light and is conscious neither of itself nor of any other being whatever except of him who through love brings about such brightness."* Maximus the Confessor

Note: (580–662) Influential monk who was convicted of heresy.

"All that I have written seems to me like straw compared with what has now been revealed to me." Thomas Aquinas

Note: After experiencing union, he abandoned writing Summa Theologiae.

Essays in Zen Buddhism
D.T. Suzuki. Published by Grove Press 1949, 2000 (B)

[the principles of Zen] *"A special transmission outside the scriptures; no dependence upon words and letters; a direct pointing to the soul of man; the seeing into one's own nature and thus the attainment of Buddhahood."* Bodhidharma

"However deep your knowledge of abstruse philosophy, it is like a piece of hair in the vastness of space; however important your experience in things of the worldly, it is like a drop of water thrown into the unfathomable abyss."
Te-shan Hsuan-chien [Tokusan Senkan]

Note: Quotations relate to the summary as a whole, rather than to any one essay.

Feel Good—Do Good

IT DOES NOT require deep psychological or spiritual insights to understand basic relationships between feeling good and doing good. When we feel good—healthy, happy, successful—we are then more likely to do good for other people. We usually do what we feel like doing, unless required to do otherwise.

Similarly, when we do good for others it frequently makes us feel good. That should not be the primary reason for helping, even if it often is an aftereffect. Both psychotherapists and religions agree that we should to "do good," the former because it makes patients feel better about themselves and the latter because it is part of the moral creed of every faith. Good intentions, alone, are not enough.

There are other aspects of feeling good and doing good which are important to both our psychological and spiritual well-being. There are "feel good" teachings of religion. If you believe that God always loves you, as most religions teach, and you love God, as all theistic faiths urge, that does feel good. Conversely, if you believe no one loves you and you cannot truly love another, then a psychotherapist might help. "Feel good" mysticism, however, is superficial at best and deceitful at worst. The goal of *feeling good* is misguided.

The capacity for doing good is seldom an objective of therapy, yet therapists recognize that the inclinations to do bad can be signs of a disturbed person. "Do unto others as you would have them do unto you" is not just a teaching of the sacred scriptures, it is also common sense. It might be simply summarized as "what goes around, comes around," an idiomatic expression of the laws of *karma*. Morality is one foundation for almost all of the traditions of mysticism, too.

Does a mystic always "feel good" and "do good?" That depends on the context. During an experience in union with the divine, it is quite sure that a mystic feels good … albeit unconsciously. In those intuitive insights which precede, and usually follow, such spiritual oneness, mystics are certain that they *must* do good. It is not only a moral teaching, or a social code, but the acceptance of the unity of all beings makes it the unquestioned right mode of conduct.

Those who pursue the mystical quest to "feel good" are deluding themselves from the outset. Unfortunately, there will be a lot of *not feeling too good* on the path to spiritual awareness. There will be much confusion: Which way to follow, how best to practice, what pitfalls to avoid, many false preconceptions, and some equally false experiences. The good feeling of being in the divine essence is only incidental to the conscious union with it. It is often felt later.

There are some who believe that "doing good" will hasten their progress toward enlightenment. No and yes. If doing good actually enhances your self-image, satisfying your ego and ennobling you as an individual, then all of your acts of goodness will not advance your quest. If your good deeds are *sacramental*, done in hopes of obeying the divine will,* and you have no other selfish motivations, they can lead you to realizing oneness with the divine.

When you feel good while doing good, or after, then it is probably not selfless action. When you do what is right because it is right, even if it requires personal sacrifice and may not feel very good at the time, you might be on the way to, for and of the divine. "I just want to be happy" is not an objective of mystics. "I want everyone to be happy" is an unrealistic goal. Happiness can result from feeling good and doing good, but should not be the motive by itself.

Learning how to "feel," deeply, is good. The feeling of divine Love, a profound emotion which can never be expressed, drives you forward on the path. Intuitive insight into divine Truth, that is felt as certainty in your mind, removes all your doubts about unity. Absorption in divine Reality, which is felt in the soul, lifts you beyond self. You feel good, yet not simply because it feels good.

Learning how to "do," ardently, is also good. It motivates you to respond to the divine will which the soul, through your conscience, tells you is right. *Doing*, even with the best of intentions, might not achieve good results. A *do-gooder* is an idealist, although sometimes naively so. You must consider that others may not agree with your concept of "good" or your sense of timing. Selfless action is a path to realization which must be tread carefully. *Goodness* is relative.

---

* Interpreting divine will is clouded by egos; people often disagree on what "God wants."

Like much of mysticism, "feel good—do good" also has paradoxes. What may feel good to you can lead away from consciousness in the divine. Doing good for the wrong reasons could stray you from the path, too. Sometimes, what is unpleasant to you at the moment may be exactly right, or what seems wrong to others might be what really needs to be done. Who said that it would be easy? If you want *easy* forget about mysticism. If you want *good* then you have a chance. *Right*, even if it may not seem good, is even better. Perplexed?

> Note: In their usage, correctly defined, good and right can have different applications.

Discard, Abandon and Realize

FEW WORDS ARE totally adequate when writing about mysticism. These essays say that you must *discard* your ego and *abandon* your individuality to *realize* the divine. What does that mean and is it possible? There may be better verbs, but let us just examine these three. It may provide the basis for our better understanding.

The ego is a concept you began to develop shortly after birth. As you matured, you molded it, fed it, nurtured it, and watched it grow. Gradually, it had begun to control much of your life. Whenever you had sought to live without it, it whined, it begged, it connived, and it refused to be left behind. The sense of *I, me* and *my* ignores the soul.

The ego became your personal identity, even if you did frequently suspect that it was shallow, corrupt and manipulative. It had often provided you with good feelings of confidence, direction and worth. Unfortunately, it had sometimes showed its insecurities, confusion and ineffectiveness, too. You cannot live life fully with it and you cannot live without it; you can discard it, occasionally.

Discard is a term used in card games when you reject one card to, hopefully, replace it with a better one. In this living game, you do not always have to play with the cards you were dealt with at birth. In mysticism, as in poker, you do not throw the ego card away, you simply place it face down on this life's table so the divine can deal you a spirit card. Let go of the ego to win with the soul.

Your individuality is that sense of uniqueness which distinguishes you from another person: your physical appearance, personality, accomplishments, and other distinct characteristics. It is usually a positive influence, still can cause isolation from other people. Some persons do suppress their own individuality by dressing, talking and behaving like those they admire. Unlike the ego, you can live with it or without it, depending on your current inclination to do so.

Abandon is surrender of control or possession and, often, the knowledge that thing which is abandoned was left to the mercy of someone else. This strict usage is quite appropriate for mysticism. First, we acknowledge that we are not truly in control and can never "possess" this life, but are interdependent on all of existence. Second, we give up the free will of our individualism to allow the divine will to guide our life from separation to union with All.

Devotees of mysticism can accept, intellectually, the absolute unity of all existence and ultimate oneness with the divine. Most other people either doubt these concepts or reject them altogether. Suddenly, consciously being in the One can transform some of the aspirants into confirmed mystics or shock a few non-believers into amazement. Each of them may emerge from that direct awareness enlightened; it might just result in their ego inflation or neurosis.

Realize is defined both to comprehend correctly or become aware completely *and* to make real or to actualize something. In incorrect usage, it could also mean attainment or achievement. The unity of existence and oneness with the divine are a present condition of all life; they are not something to be either attained or achieved, yet are usually unrealized by most people. True mystics, frequently, are correctly aware *and* do really actualize union in this life.

Realizations of divine oneness can vary in degree and duration. They are a gift, not a personal accomplishment. Your ego cannot take credit for them—although it will probably try—and your own individuality had little to do with them. They might enhance you as a person, but are experienced by more than a million people … of the billions on Earth. You had felt special just after each encounter, yet probably normal when later remembering it. And then what?

People have many special experiences, both good and bad, which come and go. Some have become fond memories and many others were repressed to avoid continued suffering. Divine union, itself, is unforgettable, although it is mostly unfathomable. When you do try to grasp its meaning, seek to retell or repeat it, it is usually lost. Appreciate it when it comes, do not despair when it leaves and *do not* try to rationalize it or hold onto it. You cannot *hold* the divine.

We may step out of this life into eternal life, but we are still *here*. Past experiences of oneness are meaningless unless they change your life *now*. Grand transformations are not required or expected, just a gradual improvement will do. Being wonderful yesterday does not make up for being the same miserable person today.

Even a good person will become a better person when conscious, here and now, of our eternal unity with the divine. We can then *be* what *is*.

Union requires intense concentration, self-sacrifice and dedicated practice. You do not *earn* it; you learn to accept what is given by grace. An absorption in universal unity may be used by the ego to proclaim your superiority in this life; then divine awareness is lost.

> Note: Ego is inflated during this transient life on Earth; it is deflated in the context of the Universe and eternal life.

Beyond Words

SOME THEOLOGIANS AND philosophers sought to interpret the sacred scriptures of their religion. A few mystics employed metaphysics to explain the significance of their experiences. Words cannot entirely convey the spiritual teachings of holy texts, nor fully depict mystical consciousness. They might, however, be useful for explaining how to integrate each into this life. At best, they are guideposts.

Many people are quite fascinated with words, as though knowing the right words can clarify everything. Unfortunately, that is seldom true. Just look in any dictionary and you will find numerous words which have multiple applications. Definitions themselves can vary between sources and, most often, between languages. The most commonly accepted meanings of words can be distinct from precise usage in any language, as a book on synonyms can elaborate.

History may modify the use and definitions of words, as classical languages do vary from modern phrasing. The context of words can change their effect, which is why short quotations can misrepresent their author's purpose. Also, too many people are careless in their choice of words. *They* know what they meant, yet the listener or reader might not. Some writers are too verbose, especially those with a broad vocabulary which may not only exceed many readers' knowledge, but can also impede their intended understanding.

Some mystics claim that we can intentionally change the impact of God's Word. They say our aspirations, prayers and invocations can influence the way that God functions, especially in relation to humankind. Others criticize those as contrivances to display powers or miracles to impress their followers. Some cynics, including a few mystics, have said that the divine does not really care what we want. The movement of the cosmos, the divine will, is totally detached from entreaties of humans or any other beings of creation.

There are people who maintain just the opposite: Our every thought, our every spoken word and our intention in every action is judged by the divine. We may build up merits and demerits daily which might influence a final judgment which will determine either our fate for eternity, or our place in the next life. For them, our words and deeds will become the critical measures of our life.

For those who believe that devotion is superior to knowledge, all the theologies, philosophies or metaphysics cannot replace love. The only words that really matter are those of prayer, poetry, song, or other stated tributes to the divine. Spiritual music and dance, meditation and contemplation can be more important than either speaking or writing. Words of love pale before our deep feelings of rapture and ecstasy. Divine love for us, which is present presently in compassionate and merciful grace, is beyond any of our expressions or full appreciation. Its breadth is endless ... always here and now.

The traditions of mysticism often use different terms for divine realizations. *Devekut* in the Kabbalah, *fana* in Sufism, *samadhi* in Hinduism, *satori* in Buddhism, and *unio mystica* in Christianity have similar connotations, until they are compared with one another. Then, proponents of each faith frequently claim theirs is superior to all others. Perpetual mystics say that divine absorption cannot be measured, nor affected, by words or concepts.

Most true mystics feel it is impossible to portray direct awareness in divine essence with words which most people could understand. Natural wonders, art, music, and the silent transmissions of serenity and bliss convey spirituality more precisely than words. Mystics entered a degree of consciousness so estranged from mortal life that verbal analogies are inadequate. Critics ridicule that as an excuse for the inability to explain something which was only imagined. Mystics respond that skeptics cannot see beyond their own ignorance.

The more mystics attempt to describe their realization of unity, or to provide the significance for it, the more they lose the immediacy, immensity and ineffability of divine union. Exegesis, bringing out the meaning, sometimes results in eisegesis, reading meaning into those experiences. Some mystics used their awareness of divine oneness for hermeneutics, i.e. interpretations of sacred scriptures. Scriptures may have led them into the mystical quest, and some passages might be read to have mystical implications, but reverse application of experiences to text could distort the original intent of those scriptures. This too frequently can cause conflicts between the views of mystics and those of their orthodox religion.

Words usually result from mental activities, although many of them do have affective content or describe material states. Union with the divine is an inseparable unity—emotional, mental, physical, *and* spiritual—involving the whole being within all of existence. Any words, even ten thousand words, are unable to totally communicate its scope. What it *is* is truly and completely beyond words.

> Note: The words oneness, union or unity, awareness, consciousness, experience, or realization are inadequate. Even "the divine" when used as a noun, is insufficient for ultimate Reality.

Oneness in Separateness

SOME PEOPLE VIEW this world in dualities: Good and evil, true and false, above and below, inside and outside, young and old, past and future, and seemingly endless pairs of opposites. A knowledgeable person realizes that there are many perspectives in between; in fact, most of us usually live in those intermediate aspects. A truly wise person can see beyond the pairs to their potentials. There may be a little good in every evil, some truths among the falsehoods, an upside to the downside, a within in the without, etc. and *vice versa*.

True mystics are aware of oneness in all. The *many* are transient manifestations of the One. Each is balanced by the other in the infinite here or offset by the other in the eternal now. What looks to be one thing there might be seen to be another elsewhere. What appeared correct yesterday may seem incorrect tomorrow. These mystics do not accept as Real any there or elsewhere, yesterday or tomorrow. They may appear real only in space and time.

Space and time are useful concepts* which we mere mortals—as temporary inhabitants of this whirling and relatively small mass called Earth—use to measure

---

* In pleasure, space expands; time flies by. In pain, space contracts; time drags on. In this life, measurable distance and duration are less important than our perception of them.

worldly life. We all actually exist here and now, although our minds often dwell on images which are spatially elsewhere or in alternate temporal spans. Our emotions and bodies, other aspects of our apparent triune being, mainly deal with here and now. Our inner self, or soul, is always here and now.

We seem apart from the world, although we always reside in this world. We are never separate from our soul, although we seldom do live in it. Mystics who live through their soul never feel detached from souls of other people, spirits of different living beings or sparks of inanimate objects which radiate from the endless divine essence. They do not experience any exclusion from physical surroundings: manifested from infinite divine matter. Also, their thoughts are not isolated from the minds of others: which are extensions of eternal divine consciousness. For them, perennial union is fact, certainty and unquestioned; diversity is simply passing appearances. They look beyond surface realities.

True mystics do not ignore separateness in *temporary* peril. In a fleeting existence as singular humans, they occupy an infinitesimal space called the body during a speck of time called this life. Most are compassionate and usually not concerned with the evils of others. Their higher regard is for the commonality, community and communion amongst all. Many of them do see this life as a partial disclosure, an incomplete manifestation or an unfinished revelation of the infinite divine. Death seems to follow an eventual decay, a terminal illness or a fatal accident in separateness from eternal life. Divine union is unfulfilled within the concepts of space and time.

Too many of the rest of men and women ignore oneness in *eternal* jeopardy. This life seems to be their only reality; satisfying this self is their primary concern. They view the evils of others as threats to them, overlooking their causes. They usually exist in an emotional, mental and physical shell, interacting with most people in their own best interests. Every year and every day is filled with attention to their selfish, personal welfare. Thoughts of death are disregarded, postponed or feared. They shape God to their preferred image and rarely, if ever, consider eternal life. They alienate themselves from divine unity and, as a result, do not realize it (and do not care to).

All of this may seem confusing. This life is confusing. We often do not know why we are here, where we are going, nor what will happen when we get there. Mystics might be confused during the process of becoming, but they have clarity while *being* in union. The divine in you, or soul, may seem obscured; there is nothing obscure while one, self and soul united, consciously lives in the divine One.

One is oneness; two is separateness. We all, in and of ourselves, are *apparently* just one of the many. In spiritual knowing, or *gnosis*, each one is inside every self, integral to the One. In devolution, which some may call creationism, the One had become the many. During evolution, the many are currently moving towards the One. Most of Judaism, Christianity and Islam view this life in linear time, with a beginning and an end. For Hinduism and some of Buddhism, life is cyclical and continuous; time repeats itself endlessly in an altered form. For true mystics, the One was, the many are and the One again will be—in space and time—and always *is* in eternity.

In mysticism, sin is while the self is separated from the divine by ignorance. We can overcome ignorance of eternal life by accepting at-one-ment with One in the All. We can close the huge gap, as seen through dualities of space and time, between our self and the transcendent divine by reuniting our self with the divine immanent in our soul. It is not *our soul*, it is an emanation of infinite, eternal divine essence that permeates all of existence, regardless of how we view the creating process. Religion and science address only parts.

Finding the Soul

MANY PEOPLE SOUGHT their soul, their true self, their innermost being. Most others, of course, have not even tried. Mystics, when beginning their quest, searched to no avail until they accepted that it is here and now. It was so obvious that they had overlooked it.

You cannot *find* the soul; it is not a place or a thing to find. The soul, however, can be experienced. Have you seemed to be judging your self? When the ego self gets angry, does the inner self wonder why? When your mind thinks strange thoughts, does the true self acknowledge that they are strange? When the self reflected in the mirror behaves badly, is the self within the mirror aware that it is wrong? It can sometimes be a painful evaluation. This self-critic is your conscience … innate, not the learned superego[*]; it is the outer edge of the soul, underlying a ripple in the divine ocean.

You cannot even realize "your soul" because it is not *yours*; it is the divine within you. From that metaphorical ocean, the divine is observing life on shore. On its surface, each soul reflects one mortal self walking on the beach we call this life. The divine essence, the inner depths shared by all souls, is usually detached from activities of worldly selves, like an audience to a play,

---

[*] Superego considers how others judge you, as learned from parents and community.

but may sometimes intervene in emergencies or to guide lost egos back onto the path.

When you do realize soul, accepting the divine influx, it can act as a spiritual guide to the manifest ego self which has a name, a shape and moves in a variety of circumstances. In this play of life, all of the characters have a part and script to keep the divine production flowing. Most of them use their theatrical persona as a mask to hide their inner uncertainty. Many of these actors just want to be stars, not in the supporting cast. Others forget their lines while thinking about personal problems. Some do not come on stage or do not act on cue, which then upsets the performance of everyone else. True mystics play their roles *soul*-fully ... exactly as directed.

Another analogy to understand soul is sports, where teamwork is more important than individual accomplishments. Many athletes want the glory of scoring, but without their teammates' assistance they might not have a chance. We are in this game of life together, although some people seem to think only of their own achievement. Soul is reaching deep inside to actuate our greatest potential, while always aware of playing in harmony with other souls. For true mystics, *winning* is living sacramentally ... in and for the divine.

Forget inadequate comparisons with this life. Consider instead eternal life. In sports, every game is over in one day and a season concludes each year. In the theater, a play will only run for a limited number of stagings ... albeit for many years. Do we move from one human life to another, or from this mortal being through levels of ethereal being, in search for the divine? Infinity has no boundaries or limits; it is the infinite *here*. Eternity has no beginning or end; it is the eternal *now*. Here and now are not only important in this life, they are two vital aspects of the spiritual life which lives endlessly in all of us. It is the divine One here and now manifested in All. Look beyond space and time.

Finding the soul, even if that was possible, is less significant than living in the soul. Most of us live in our immediate emotions, our extended minds and our ever present bodies until death. Few of us live through the soul, constantly aware of the divine essence in us. It is the spiritual life which gives true purpose to our human lives. It is spiritual life which continues after this brief stay on Earth. It is the spirit in each of us which unites us with the spirit in All: all people, all sentient beings, all seemingly inanimate objects, *and* the divine.

Is divine union a broad expansion of mind or the spiritual string which binds material life together? In metaphors, both *and partly*. When cosmic consciousness, *or only yours*, is completely aware of universal matter, *or that which you can perceive,* they transform into One divine essence, or *that essence you can be aware of in this life*. When that divine essence is manifested, it is partially apparent as matter and consciousness, *including you*. Does this describe the eternal cycle of existence and the evident, however temporary, thing we call this life? Who knows? Knowing is not being. Who can understand? Understanding will not bring it. You do not need either to *be* it. Be that which is, not just what you think it is.

Mystical oneness is a not full consciousness of this Universe and becoming the divine. It is universal consciousness felt while sharing in divine unity. This is not a faith or belief; it is the certainty of direct experience. When this realization is maintained, even at the time of mortal passing, we no longer cling to worldly desires and will continue in immortal bliss. The sense of ego self and separate individuality are forgotten to rest in that peace of the eternal and infinite One. Our apparent beginning and becoming then cease in the Reality of *being*. This is the greatest achievement in life.

> Note: This essay is not based on books; it was suggested in talks with ten mystics.

A Little of This, a Little of That

A SUMMARY IS "a little of this, a little of that." Here it is a sampling of mystical traditions in the five major religions, with an overview of their approaches, highlighting many of the similarities and some differences. You do not, however, become enlightened by dabbling.

Too many devotees jump from one religion to another, alternate from going it alone to studying with a spiritual teacher, and/or move from one guru to the next in search of the one true way. There is no "one true way"; there are now about seven billion *ways*. You must probe the depths of your inner self; other people can only guide you on the path. The trials and experiences along the way will vary.

It is a seeking unlike studying at a university, where you attend a variety of courses as taught by many different instructors. You can join a spiritual community, go on retreat with others, be alone at home, or stay in isolation in the wilderness, here or abroad. Divine realization does not depend on *where you are*, it is only possible when you truly accept *who you are*. It is the true nature of being.

"Who am I?" The everyday answer is "a little of this and a little of that." Do not consider your ordinary life, with its fleeting emotions, confusing thoughts and necessary bodily actions. A pastor, therapist or a physician can assist you with most of those problems. Realizing your spiritual essence may be a solitary task, but you are never at it alone. Every person, every living being, every object is involved in the same quest; a few are aware of it, yet most of them are unaware.

Even if you do stay with one religion throughout your search, and study with one spiritual teacher for many years, you will still try a little of this and a little of that. Each faith has many approaches to mystical consciousness and aspirants seldom find the right path on their first choice. Qualified teachers usually integrate a variety of methods for each student—according to their levels of dedication, abilities and awareness—gradually changing them as they progress.

For most seekers, and for most mystics, it is necessary to balance a little of this life with a little of the eternal life. Emotionally, we cannot be so devoted to divine Love that we neglect to love our family and friends. Mentally, our thoughts cannot be so concentrated on divine Truth that we overlook those many truths about mundane living. Physically, we cannot to be so absorbed in divine Reality that we ignore everyday realities. Or *vice versa*.

A little of that eternal life should be integrated into a little of this life. If our spiritual insights are limited to periods of meditation or contemplation, they might temporarily enlighten us but they will not transform us. The perpetual mystics, who some call saints, have been completely transformed in every aspect of their being. They live in the divine every moment. Our learning must be incorporated into our being if we are to progress toward eternal oneness.

"A little goes a long way." Add a few drops of red wine to a glass of water and all of the liquid turns pink. Add a few drops of divine insight to this life and you begin to live in that glow. While it may be a waste of fine wine, it is an excellent use of the soul. Most doctors say that drinking a glass of red wine each day is good for your heart. Most of the spiritual teachers recommend that we drink in a little divine spirit daily to add *heart* to our lives. It enhances our being.

Few things in life are all this or all that; most are a little alike or a little different. Your inner self is the spiritual essence of the eternal life; your unconscious mind hides repressed memories of this life. Both are usually not in our consciousness, yet can be reawakened to affect daily living. Surface soul is like this self's reflection in the divine; conscience opens soul's depths to reflect the divine essence in this self's life. It may be controversial, but still worth considering.

"Forget little, I want big! Grand periods of enlightenment with bright light! Immediate transformation to a godlike being on Earth! A guaranty engraved in stone of eternal life!" That idle daydream is never going to happen in this life. Divine realization comes little by little, although at times in clear moments of insight. Love the divine in all to live in divine Love, weigh all "truths" to become aware of divine Truth, deal with each reality to discover divine Reality.

You may graduate from a university with a degree. Intuitive insights will gradually lead you to the divine, with different degrees of consciousness. Brief direct experiences themselves will increase your insights into this life and then allow you to live intuitively in the divine here and now. By bringing the inner spirit outside, your outer daily living reveals what is inherent within. A little of that hidden, true being will create a lot more of this apparent becoming.

Living a little better life today, and adding a little more spirit every day, will eventually become eternal life in the divine.* We are already in the divine, infinitely and eternally, but must consciously experience it, actuate it and be in that awareness in this life. It is to be presently in the Reality which is present in all transient realities.

---

* Divine life is not to be studied, prayed for or dreamt; it is to be lived here and now.

Heads Up!

AS AN IDIOM, "heads up" means to watch for danger. Hyphenated, "heads-up" is a suggestion to be more aware. Some individuals go through life with their heads down,* literally as well as figuratively. They may be "ducking for cover" or, more frequently, are just lost in themselves. The fog of their ego causes ignorance about life itself.

All of us, occasionally, do walk with our heads down while we are engrossed in our thoughts. Today, too many of us might walk—or drive—with our heads up when talking on our cell phones. In either case, and as a result, we are less conscious of our surroundings here and what is happening now. That can be dangerous; it can also limit both our human and spiritual awareness. We must have our "heads up"—in this place at this time—to live life fully and divinely, too.

When mothers say "mind your manners" they mean to be aware of how we behave, usually because other people are watching. *Mindfulness* is one basic principle of Buddhist practice, especially during meditation. They should not only sit with their body erect—meditators with their heads down may be asleep—they must also maintain an awareness of the flow of their sentiments,

---

* Bow your head in prayer, but not to get "ahead" in this life or to realize eternal life.

thoughts and sensations. They then realize that all of them are impermanent.

Psychotherapists often urge mindfulness to their patients, they might call it self-analysis, to be cognizant of the motives for their actions and to become aware of the unconscious reasons for their thoughts and emotions. Therapists themselves must be mindful not only of what their clients say, with their words and/or their body, but also their probable unconscious or unexpressed motivations. Practitioners must keep their own personal problems in abeyance.

When a physician asks for your symptoms, you must be mindful of what your body is telling you. Your auto mechanic will say the same about your car. When we do not have our "heads up" about our life as lived, we cannot know how to improve it. Some spiritual persons speak of heads up literally; they say that they feel more at one with the world while their head is lifted, while either standing, walking or sitting. That is often quite effective, yet it is not always easy to do.

"Pay attention!" is a more forceful idiom than heads up. We could be aware someone has entered the room, still must be attentive to recognize who that person is. Mystical realization is frequently said to be an *awareness* of the divine. Attentiveness is integrating that awareness into our active consciousness in daily living. By literal definition, *attentive* means both "paying attention; observant" and "mindful of the well-being of others; considerate."

In the latter usage, attentiveness means to keep our heads up to the needs of others. Earth revolves on its axis; the world does not revolve around "me." Whether it be politically, financially, socially, or even psychologically, other people are more important to all of this life than our individual, ego self. Spiritually, the divine essence does pervade all of existence. Soul is in every person, which unites them with all other people and all of existence always.

To "clear your head" means to become more attentive to what is happening around you. To "clear your mind" is to become more conscious or aware of what is going on inside you. A *clear mind* will better see the oneness in all; a muddled mind will only see "me" and "them," often without understanding either. A heads-up attitude could describe someone who has a positive outlook and is open to new ideas. Both attributes are required on the mystical quest.

We can "bury our heads in the sand" and then be oblivious to both what is happening all around us and inside us. Seekers sometimes "head down the wrong road" and are "headed for disappointment," because their head will be filled with erroneous views and practices. A few people do "lose their heads" on the path, both past martyrs and the insane. Mysticism is confusing; English is almost as bad: there at least 40 meanings or uses for the word "head."

Heads-up could also mean to live for this moment, here and now. Too often, our minds are rehashing the past or anticipating the future; meanwhile the present is not attended to properly. What we do *right here, right now* becomes a memory of the past and impacts the future. Done poorly, life as lived today would end in becoming a "has-been," or will continue as a "wannabe," without accomplishing a lot. The divine is in us; we must be actively in the divine.

Devotees might ask, or want to ask, their spiritual teacher "am I making any headway on the path?" If you need to ask the question, of your mentor or yourself, then the answer is probably "not too much." Divine consciousness is not "all in your head"; it must be in your heart and in your actions as well. To be aware of unity, with all existence and the divine, is a crucial advancement on your quest. To attentively make it a part of your life, feeling oneness every moment and living in and for the divine, will answer every question.

> Note: "Here and now" should mean everywhere and always; only saints live like that.

The Grand Excuse

"THE DEVIL MADE me do it." Whether this is said tongue-in-cheek, or by a believer in satanic influences, it is still *the grand excuse*. Too many people attempt to blame someone else for their own troubles or lack of personal achievement. If you want to see the devil, simply look at what is reflected in the mirror. Blaming yourself, even when it is justified, is quite difficult. "It isn't my fault," they usually say.

It is equally wrong for you to fault yourself for every misfortune and shortcoming. You can become your own devil when you allow the demons of your mind to rule your life. There are guilty people; others are ridden by guilt. All humans make mistakes; a few believe themselves to be hopeless. Each of us fail at some tasks; some persons feel doomed to failure. The psychologically impaired must ask for help or allow their maladies to be *the grand excuse*.

When tragedy impacts their life, some people reproach God. "How could *He* let this happen?" "My God failed me." "If this can happen on Earth there is no God in heaven." Unfortunately, too many religious leaders respond with sayings like "God works in mysterious ways" or "there must be a reason in God's plan." Most Hindus and Buddhists may point to *karma*, the consequences of our previous actions in this life or the last. While the latter might seem more reasonable than the former, they can both be types of *the grand excuse*. We too frequently want to excuse ourselves today and/or to wallow in self-pity. It is much easier to accuse another.

The grand excuse, or many variations thereof, is typically given for the reason not to seek divine oneness. "It is impossible to do." "I do not have the time to try." "I have given up trying." So, these persons go on with their lives, conceding their limitations, finding partial satisfactions, wishing to avoid being blamed, and ending with a long list of failures. In many cases, at death those people have accepted that they will not go to heaven. They are usually right. Depending on their religious convictions, or personal beliefs, they may be born again to seek elusive perfection, go to a *purgatory* to work out their sins or, perhaps, pass on into oblivion. Lives are different; why not afterlives? Beliefs might become true.

Christianity offers a grand *a priori* excuse: we all are born in sin due to the fall of Adam. Many men accuse Eve. Eve blamed the serpent. The serpent isn't talking unless you let it. Some Hindus call this serpent the *kundalini*, spiritual energy coiled in the base of the spine, which must first be released through the crown of the head, in greater consciousness, to reunite with the divine. Separation is *the grand excuse* of most religions; mystics realize it is just imagined. The mystical "truth" is that All is in One and One is in All here and now, in infinite and eternal Reality. Every person must actualize divine union in this life and then live in that awareness to be in eternal life in the divine. Your excuses can prevent that realization.

Get over it! Forget the excuses, even if some of them are valid. Forge ahead with what you can do. Try your damndest or you might be damned. If someone offers a simple and foolproof way to realize the divine life, either that person is attempting to fool you or you are a fool to believe it. As the Dalai Lama once stated, "No one said that it would be easy." The mystical path is a maze; mystical consciousness is amazing. You may get lost on the path, move off of it entirely or find yourself back where you started. Aha! That is the answer. You are always where you started in the here-now (not space-time). Divine union is forever here and now; your deepest, most hidden, elusive self—the soul—is already living in the divine.

Many people might say, "that sounds too basic," especially those who have spent years seeking in books, in prayer or meditation, and/or traveling across the globe without much apparent success. Again, this is *the grand excuse.** Just because your previous efforts have been in vain does not mean that you should reject the obvious. Most devotees of mysticism believe that the divine is in their soul, if only they could find their soul. Look at who is seeking, behind the masks, underlying the surface self and all its contortions on Earth. Forget conceptions of "you"; allow the divine within to guide this life. What *is* already is. You must "realize" it: make it real in the present, embrace this One vital essence, always aware of the divine inherent in All, actively conscious that All

---

* If you deny, reject or overlook what is, ignorance is no longer your grand excuse.

are One in transcendent *and* immanent unity. That is the greatest achievement in this life.

Some people might say that these criticisms are too harsh. Maybe so. Perhaps we should not take responsibility for our own emotions, thoughts and actions. We should just accept rejection and loss, not be conscious of divine Love. We should not maintain an awareness of divine Truth while living. We should not try to overcome adversities to actualize divine Reality. We should merely hope for little loves, temporary truths and what seems real for the moment. While you stayed closed within this life, you cannot open to eternal life. The greatest achievement, living in oneness, then seems impossible.

Contemporary Views

MANY CONTEMPORARY MYSTICS are laypeople who seldom speak about religion, although most are quite religious. Mysticism, for them, is considered a mode of being, not a question of their faith.

These people are not trying to convince you or asking you to agree with what they say. They are merely attempting to explain their own direct awareness. They have no desire to describe their mystical experiences. Application to living is far more important. It is all-embracing discernment.

Almost every person feels that their life is lacking in some way, although they are seldom able to define it. There always seems to be *something missing*. True mystics feel *wholeness* often. It is not a temporary absorption in divine union. Rather, it is identifying with the divine essence everywhere. Living, for them, usually expands beyond their own immediate sentiments, thoughts and sensing.

"Just let it be." Many mystics today have said that, in various ways. We frequently do try to control our lives. To some extent that is possible. Much of what happens, however, is beyond our control. *Acceptance* is a positive spin on *surrender*. We must accept what is, or actively change it to something better. Mark Twain said "the worst things in my life never happened," yet caused needless worry. Conversely, the best things in life often occur without any planning or expectations. Dealing with what *is* should be our priority. We must live in the present, rather than dwell on the past or the future.

Existence is not just a mental exercise, despite what some Eastern schools of mysticism may seem to imply. There are emotional and physical factors of equal importance, which might be stressed too much in the West. For mystics, mind and body, and their emotive interaction, are less significant than the spiritual essence underlying them. A mind without spirit would be lethargic; a body without spirit would be ailing; lacking spirit in both can actually cause physical death. Life is not only becoming, it is being here and now.

Rebirth is conceived as being born in another body, after death in this life. For "born again" Christians, it is reaffirmation of their faith while still alive. Contemporary mystics sometimes speak of being born again. After absorption in oneness, they view existence from a broader perspective. The universal essence, which had engulfed them, is later felt as background to everything they experience. Living has greater purpose,* even if they cannot explain it in words. Realizing eternal life is present currently, they do not fear death.

Religions today usually concentrate on earthly being, within the confines of space and time. They seldom mention either mysticism or eternity. Many books about Judaism, Christianity and Islam omit their mystical

---

* Their feeling, thinking and actions become for the soul, the whole and all, not for "I, me" and "my." Their sense of being reaches beyond limited personal concerns.

tradition. Much current literature by Buddhists only touch on the Dharmakaya or Nirvana. The mystical quest for unity is still a vital part of Hindu movements, but most people in modern India are now more concerned with secular interests.

Many mystics disassociate themselves from orthodox beliefs and practices, which is resented by many of their religion's members. Some reinterpret the scriptures and prophesies of their faith, which upsets some of its leaders. The priorities of mystical traditions are frequently at odds with the mainstream of their institutional faith. They concentrate on the *eternal here and now*, partially manifested in space and time, yet also transcendent to each and both.

"What about eternal life?" Most people who even consider it may regard it as after passing on. It can, however, be realized both consciously and presently. What we call *this life* might be just like watching and performing in a play on stage. The concluded acts we call the past. The following acts, termed the future, have yet to be presented. For true mystics, here ... now ... this moment is Reality. It is not merely an intermission. It is truly boundless and endless.

Many of these essays use symbolic terms, as did most quotations of mystics. "How do they relate to everyday living?" If you looked at a movie film (not digital), frame by frame, you would not grasp the meaning of the complete picture. When you look at this life, hour by hour, day by day, you cannot see it in its whole context. Even if you could review one mortal life in its entirety, its greater spiritual significance would be missing. Life is all of existence.

"How can one person possibly relate to all of existence, let alone to the spiritual essence which underlies it?" That is what mystics are conscious of, sometimes momentarily and, rarely, throughout every day. "Can you believe in a personal God and be a mystic?" Most of them do. "Can you be an atheist and a mystic?" A few are. God is the supreme concept of that essence which is *God beyond God*.

"God is a concept and not a reality?" God is as real as you want God to be. The divine essence is Reality, even if you do not believe in God. It is another mystical paradox. "Why can't it be simple?" It is simple … it simply *is*. It is our minds which add the complexity.

Beyond Me

"**IT IS BEYOND ME.**" How many times have we said that when we cannot understand something, especially when another person acts in a way which appears to defy common sense? As self-conscious human beings, however, it is often difficult—if not impossible—to get beyond "me." We usually *seem* captive to an ego which is with us in our every thought. It does not, however, have to rule our lives.

What are some techniques for discarding the ego and abandoning individuality? Be objective, not subjective. To control sentiments of "I," weigh *reactions* to your words, others' *sensitivity* to your thoughts and probable *consequences* of your actions. To heighten thinking beyond "me," be cognizant of the *reasons* for your reasoning, *goals* of your learning, *relevance* of your memories, and real *possibilities* in your imagining. To enhance your senses beyond "my," *look* not just see, *listen* not only hear, *feel* not solely touch, identify the *scent* not merely smell, and *savor* not taste alone. Go outside "self," beyond me. The inherent significance of what is presently here is external.

A complementary method is to concentrate on the moment, not ruminate about the past. When you repeatedly recall anything, it is usually in relation to you. While concentrating, "you" is overlooked in considering "it." Art is appreciated for its beauty and technique, not merely in its value to you. Music is enjoyed for its melody and performance, not solely as a reminder of your past. Food is relished for its flavor and preparation, not simply in appeasing hunger. Each object is admired for itself, not in regard to its usefulness to you. The intrinsic importance of what is present now is transpersonal.

Are you aware of how often you have reached "beyond me?" In an emergency, when another person is at risk, you react without any thoughts of your self. When your favorite team is on verge of victory, you think only of them, not me (unless you placed a bet). In love, your concentration is on the other person. Even your pet can command attention beyond self. Life is better outside the shell.

In much of this life, our greatest happiness, satisfactions and priorities are frequently beyond any thought of "me." The list varies for each of us each day. Who says that we cannot discard our ego? Looking beyond me[**] is possible in all places, at all times. We all enjoy fine weather, are pleased by the delights of loved ones, take pride in accomplishments of our organization, and are fascinated by extraordinary events. Being beyond me can be very rewarding.

When we reflect on our troubles, unfulfilled desires and failures it is *I, me* and *my* of the ego bemoaning this life. When we compare our situation with the helpless and hopeless state of many other people, however, life

---

[**] Most repetitive or casual actions are without thoughts of "me," unless they go wrong.

seems better than we thought. Conversely, the pleasant glow of our achievements, our possessions, or completing a nice vacation can be dimmed when we consider the much greater lives of some other persons. We are not quite as wonderful as we had believed. In either case, we have then gotten beyond me.

"I am an individual" … and so you are. One human among the more than seven billion on Earth. One brown eyed among three billion. One of millions in your nation. One of many in any single category. A unique individual? Perhaps, if compared to any one other unique individual, but not among the world's entire population. Our own individuality is an identity we cling to because we were taught to do so, not because of its true significance. This life is crucial … until you die. Then others' vivid memories of you will quickly fade into only vague remembrances, unless your accomplishments were recorded in history as monumental. The world goes on, with or without you.

Absorption in *I*, *me* and *my* is not just selfish, it is not important. How you feel, what you think, and how you look have less concern to others than how they feel, what they think and how they look. Narcissism, excessive love or admiration of oneself, is something we each deny; we are all guilty of conceit, pride and vanity more often than we admit. If we only realized how seldom, how briefly or how superficially other people think about us, our ego bubble would burst. This tiny balloon called "me" is lost in the sky they are watching.

True mystics found that as they probed the depths of their inner self, beyond the surface "me," they gradually became more aware of the spirit in everyone and everything around them. The faint divine light slowly brightened to remove their own interior shadows, then diffused to illuminate and energize all of this life. *I* morphed into *we, me* to *us* and *my* to *our* as they awakened to the all-pervading essence of the divine. The cloud of ignorance lifted to reveal they were already "beyond me" every moment. Mundane living became more "alive" than ever before. Infinite existence is here … eternal life is now. In that awareness, past and future lose their significance.

Most people do not want to be "beyond me" because they are too lazy, too uncertain, or too afraid of losing what has seemed to make them unique in this life. Considering eternity is beyond them.

Beyond Other

WHEN WE DO discard our ego, and abandon our individuality, we begin to see this world as it is. This is a "seeing" beyond emotional, mental and sensory perceptions. It must even surpass "empathy," our identification with and understanding of another's situation, feelings and motives. It progresses to an intuitive insight into the spiritual essence in all around us. It is suprarational consciousness.

To completely go beyond "me" is to lose all awareness of *self*. In encounters with others you are totally absorbed in them. After selflessly following the spiritual disciplines, you will eventually lose any awareness of *other*. In sublime discernment, separate forms will appear, but essential differences do not. It is the full acceptance of oneness, sharing in divine union. The unity of existence is evident.

Many of us have had a brief absorption in universal unity, with no sense of separateness. Unless we were advanced in spirituality, or actively engaged on the mystical quest, the awe of oneness which had we felt was as inexplicable as it was profound. It was impossible to sustain it when we tried to understand it; sometimes it may even have been frightening. We had seemed to have lost hold of "reality." We actually had a glimpse of true Reality, the nature of being itself.

Some might say that to suggest going *outside self* and *outside other* contradicts traditional teachings of mysticism: to go within to seek our inner self, or the soul. Rational consciousness, with its constant imaging, conceives of outer or inner. In suprarational consciousness of mystics, it is focusing beyond apparent realities to the underlying Reality. Whether we follow the inner path of contemplation and meditation, or an outer path of objectivity and concentration, the goal is transcending appearances to realize the One essence in All.

Barriers to the inner path are an endless stream of our subjective thoughts. Blockades to the outer path are the multitude of physical objects. Our ego creates those interior barriers; our individuality experiences the external blockades. When you discard the first, and abandon the second, you can then move in any direction from the apparent to the Real. Those thoughts and objects do not vanish; their disparities are insignificant in light of shared divine essence.

Dualities of subject and object, which our isolated self does seem to encounter, are scattered reflections of the divine, diffusion of the One into the many, simply phased impressions of unity. "Darken" differences until they fade, the inner way, or "illuminate" them until sameness emerges, the outer way, each result in a vision of oneness. While in divine union, however, there are no distinctions between the lover and beloved, knower and known, or seeker and sought.

Those rare saints, who are perpetually in universal consciousness, are not interested in an inner way or outer way; those concepts just confuse what *is*. Their prime concern is accepting the flow of divine essence into every aspect of their being. Some saints again slipped into what Christian mysticism has called "the dark night of the soul," which they consider a stage just before divine union. For someone who had realized, figuratively, the fifth power (c^5) of consciousness, this return to separation from the divine One could be devastating.

Many mystics are accustomed to experiences of divine oneness coming and going; some frequently and others rarely. Those were wonderful moments which enhanced their lives. For the perpetual mystics, union was their life. Most of those saints had developed the personal fortitude which allowed them to move on until direct awareness again swept over them. They completely accepted that unity was all: in all places, at all times, infinite and eternal.

Deep meditation can result in the absence of any sense of self and other, which Hindus and Buddhists may call *samadhi*. All ordinary people experience subject and object in daily life. Most mystics are aware of essential union in spirit, yet experience the certainty of separate appearances in their lives. Saints, while aware of separate appearances, experienced the certainty of oneness and actualized that realization during every moment of their mortal living.

Do only perpetual mystics move on to *eternal* oneness? Anyone can, although there are many speculations on how. Some mystics felt that the critical time, which determines our destiny, is at the very moment of our physical death.* The soul might be reborn into another

---

* Forget waiting! Those who did not give up self during this life will not do so at death.

body or move to another plane of existence, depending on your awareness and/or religious beliefs. Elevation to eternal union will depend upon your total acceptance of unity as you pass on.

Most true mystics feel that eternal union is assured when you give up self during this lifetime. Sufis say, "to die before one dies." The Christian mystics call it "death of self." Kabbalists refer to it as *bittul ha-yesh*, "annihilation of the desiring self." Whenever there is no observing "self" then, in transpersonal actuality, there is no "other." In self-less living, all is experienced as unity in essence. The greatest achievement in life is maintaining that realization.

Wake Up!

MOST PEOPLE MOVE through this life not fully awake. They are living without making full use of their emotions, mind and body. We must wake up to move on from this life—with all its limitations—to the divine life, which is limitless. That *moving on* can be here and now.

Emotionally, many persons have difficulty suppressing their anger or disappointment, yet are unable to completely convey love or joy. Mentally, most people use less than 20% of their brain's capability, except in a crisis; much of their mind remains underused. Physically, they seldom develop the full capacity of their bodies. Insufficient exercise, poor nutrition or inadequate medical care prevent them from attaining their physical peak. Few live with their whole being.

Wake up!, here, means to realize your full potential. The three *apparent* aspects of our being—emotional, mental and physical—can be complemented and enhanced by the spiritual. For some people, "spiritual" is a vague concept with no real meaning. To "have spirit," however, is a term we recognize as a person who is vibrant, "alive" and dynamic. How can that describe any mystic, let alone a saint? Forget common conceptions. Many of them were highly spirited, very involved in life and forcefully expressed their opinions.

Their propensity for speaking out often got mystics and saints in trouble with prevailing, orthodox religious authorities. Anyone who has courage to give up their *self*, by discarding ego and abandoning individuality, is a person who has great inner strength. They speak Truth as it is, not the little "truths" their historical standards usually accepted. They feel unconditional Love without constraint, not with the circumspect conditions of their immediate culture. They live in the Reality that is, not in what their personal situation would more readily permit. They look beyond limited, everyday appearances.

Awake means to become alert, aware or cognizant. Perpetual mystics were alert to the distinctions between loving "someone" and divine Love, aware of differences between transient "truths" and absolute Truth, and cognizant of disparities between the apparent and the Real. With regard to the ground of being, they were seldom asleep ... as most people are. They often felt that their institutional religion confined them, its faithful and itself with a long list of dogmas, doctrines, prohibitions, and rules, *and let them know it.*

Examine the personal lives of some of the prominent mystics and you will find many quite colorful characters. Hui-neng of Buddhism, George Fox of Christianity, Sri Ramakrishna of Hinduism, Mansur al-Hallaj of Islam, and the Bal Shem Tov of Judaism were some of the most outspoken proponents of the mystical path. They cared little about convention and sometimes outraged leaders of their orthodox faith. George Fox, the Quaker founder, was imprisoned often; Hallaj was brutally executed. Some of the others suffered condemnation or banishment. Their mundane life was not easy.

Mystics usually were—and today are—practical, highly intelligent people dedicated to their faith. Judaism's Abraham Isaac Kook, Islam's Sir Muhammad Iqbal, Hinduism's Sri Aurobindo Ghose, Christianity's Thomas Merton, and Buddhism's 14th Dalai Lama were both esteemed within and respected outside their religion. Although few of them spoke of it, some world leaders and business luminaries were mystics. Many mystics were common persons who lived with little fanfare. Generalities do not apply, past or present.

There have been, and still are, many outstanding female mystics. Christianity: Julian of Norwich, Bridget of Sweden, Hildegard of Bingen, Teresa of Avila, Evelyn Underhill, and Bernadette Roberts. Hinduism: Lalla, Mirabai, Anandamayi Ma, Sri Ma of Kamakhya, Anandi Ma, and Amritanandamayi Ma. Islam: Rabi'a al-Adawiyya, Lubaba the Devotee, Sha'wana, Nana Asma'u, Hatice Hanim, and Hagga Zakiyya. Buddhism: Patacara, Ma.geig Lab.sgron, Mugai Nyodai, Dipa Ma, and Daw Yusanda. These are a few exemplars.

Although there have been—and currently are—ascetics who have lived solitary lives of mortification, e.g. Christian hermits and Hindu *sadhus*, that was not true of most mystics. Prayer and self-surrender increased their capacity for love and compassion. Contemplation and meditation honed their cognitive skills. *Hatha* yoga or other physical exercises toned their bodies. Spirituality, intuiting divine essence in all, enhanced their felt awareness. Their whole being was optimized to its greatest potential within the embrace of the divine.

True mystics made sacrifices and efforts with the dedication of others who have succeeded in life despite overwhelming odds. The "gift of grace" must be accepted; it is not automatic. You have to prepare yourself to realize it, then allow it to transform your being to live in the divine. It is not a professional certificate or a university degree, it must be actuated daily. It is a quite unique mode of living *beyond* most normal perceptions, expanding everyday experiencing, unlimited in scope and substance. It is seeing what *is* here and now.

> Note: "Sadhu" is an ascetic holy person. "Hatha" is for physical and mental health.

Outside the Box

IF YOU ARE to truly understand mysticism, and integrate it into your life, you must learn how to feel, think and act "outside the box." You cannot remain within the confines of traditional notions or the commonly accepted ways of approaching this world. Escape from that prison! The divine life is without constraints or limitations.

The imagery here is quite appropriate. What if you had to make all your decisions about living while detained in a jail cell? The cells may be open for brief periods each day, but the prisoners are still surrounded by walls. There are also walls around cells of everyday life. We are restricted by our ability to control our emotions, mind and body. Even with full command of our "self," we must live within the restraints of Nature and society. *Freedom* is relative.

"Free will" is really quite limited, despite belief that we control ourselves and our lives. We might think we have endless choices … until we try to make them. Each decision must not only be based on what we "want to do," but also on our own capabilities and what is expected of us. Nature and society imprison us, whether we like it or not. The key to release is mystical realization. All in One and One in All, the divine unity, opens the gate between a universal consciousness and most people's constrained awareness.

When you live outside the box of everyday life, even momentarily, you become aware of how those around you are confined. It is like being the only sober person at a cocktail party. You might not have as much fun now, but you will certainly feel a lot better tomorrow. Breaking out of mundane sentiments, worldly thoughts and mortal body enables you to view life more objectively. You see things as they are, not just through the haze of intoxicated egoism or partying individuality. True Reality is much more impressive than "realities."

The feeling of being "boxed in" is common. Sometimes we feel that our emotions are ruling our life, at least for the moment, even though we know that they ought not. At other times our endless thoughts seem to be in command, when we should be doing what is required. Our body often holds us back from complete living; we are too hungry, too tired and/or too sick to perform our best. We frequently become our own jailer. Mystics can break free.

Outer walls are the boxes of Nature and of society. Inclement weather, lack of sunlight, gravity, and/or other natural phenomena may restrain our movements. Our own *natural* aptitudes, practiced talents and learned skills are always lacking in some areas. *Human nature* is controlled mostly by society. What we believe that other people expect of us greatly influences how we feel, think and act. Considering the reactions of our family, friends, business associates, community, and/or nation determines much of what we do. Those "laws" of Nature and society govern our lives, usually more so than we wish. Mystical awareness can allow us to obey divine law here and now.

Mysticism is not an escape from this life, it is learning how to live fully while still in this prison. "Escape," whether you call it *baqa, moksha, nirvana,* or some other word, usually comes after this life for those who are enlightened. Some might say "life is hell" and, in a figurative sense, they could be right. Even the most enjoyable lives have their share of sorrows, troubles and suffering. Spiritual life, while living it, is never completely liberated from all restrictions or fluctuations; it is, however, a great deal more fulfilling. The divine life is true liberation. It is freedom from our normal sense of limits.

Feeling, thinking and acting "outside the box" might mark you as radical, a revolutionary or—to some within religions—a heretic. Just because others might not understand mystical awareness does not mean that it is wrong. It merely means that they cannot see through the cloud of ignorance which surrounds most people. True mystics are able to live in the radiance of divine Love, in the certainty of divine Truth and the unity of divine Reality. They were not *chosen*; they chose to learn of it, experience it and actuate it in their lives.

There is more to life than this life; must I die to know it? No and yes. No, you do not have to perish from the Earth ... at least, not yet. You do have to let your "self" die; the concept and feeling of self is what separates you from the rest of existence and from the essence of the divine. You are not separate from either in ultimate Reality, but do not realize that in daily realities. You can live inside boxes of sentiments, thoughts and actions, within the boxes of Nature and society, or you can step out of those *perceived* boundaries.

In the divine life—during this life—those boxes themselves do not disappear. They are discerned simply as temporary shells, rather than jail cells. You are then conscious that the divine essence flows within, over, beyond, through, and around them. You feel that in every aspect of your being: each sentiment, each thought and each action reflects that divine light. Your worldview becomes universal, encompassing a wholeness which transcends individual differences.

> Note: "Do we become saints?" Who asked that question? Aha! There is the ego again.

OTHER CONSIDERATIONS

Divine Laity

SERVING THE DIVINE is the main concern, in thought and occupation, of clergy, monks, nuns, and spiritual teachers. Many mystics live as laity in secular society. They are *in* this world, but not *of* this world.

In Buddhism, especially within the Theravada tradition, some lay people don a monk's or nun's robe and lifestyle for a few weeks or months, usually in their early twenties. It is regarded as preparation for adulthood and to confer merit on their families. Many Buddhist, Christian and Hindu monks and nuns did return to a secular life, while some laity first entered monasteries later in their lives. Most mystics, however, were never monastics nor withdrew from society.

In both the Kabbalah of Judaism and Sufism of Islam, many mystics are married, have children and adopted secular careers. Asceticism* or a monastic life are alien to them. They might meet frequently with others who follow the mystical path, still their daily life could *appear* to be similar to laity in any religion. In Hinduism, the personal search for divine union often comes in the third stage of life, after their student days and lives as a householder.

---

* Asceticism was common among some Sufis and kabbalists in the Middle Ages.

There are, of course, converts from all religions who had found their faith lacking in true spirituality and began the mystical quest in another context. Many had become quite satisfied with their new spiritual "home"; others became disillusioned and returned to the faith of their families. You cannot generalize about lives or paths of mystics. People who give up ego and individuality are quite unique.

There are mystics who have no committed religious affiliation, seldom attend a house of worship and rarely read scriptural texts. Their dedication and devotion to an absolute unity of being, even if it is not defined, is no less—and perhaps more—than many of those people who wave the flag of their orthodox faith. They actually live a spiritual life, rather than merely professing one. There are also a few mystics among confirmed atheists; "not God, but One."

Some people of other faiths may be more spiritual than many followers of the major religions. Japan has 80 million practitioners of ancient Shinto (2.8 million for "folk Shinto"). Tenrikyo, founded in the 19th century, has two million members. Also, there are active traditions among Native Americans, on both continents, dedicated believers in tribal faiths of Africa (Yoruba has more than 44 million practitioners), and among indigenous peoples of the North and South Pacific. There are distinct movements in the Caribbean and across the world. Most nations do have a variety of religious belief.

Those other faiths do not speak of "mystics" as is defined in these essays; some of them claim to have shamans, who are said to be mediums for heavenly and earthly spirits, e.g. Shinto kami. Many of their founders and leaders were "possessed of the spirit," but not in the negative sense often persecuted during the history of some major religions. Their unitary sense was as great as most mystics described here; the devotion of their followers is just as intense.

Traditionalists say that there can be no mystics in modern times. Our lives are too complex for anyone to seek mystical awareness, let alone to realize divine union. In fact, there are probably more mystics today than at any time in history. The percentages may be less, but world population is considerably greater. Some of them have not been acknowledged yet. There is no census on mystics.

Just look at the past. Meister Eckhart, one of the most influential Christian mystics, was forgotten for almost 500 years. Abulafia, a great kabbalist of the 13th century, had his works first published in the 19th century. In their life both were labeled as heretics. There are examples of mystics in every religion whose accomplishments and importance was not recognized until long after their passing.

Mystics range from rare saints, who have lived perpetually in the divine, to those millions of people who had momentary experiences of oneness. Dag Hammarskjold, former Secretary General of the U.N., Vaclav Havel, past President of the Czech Republic, Ramesh Balsekar, CEO of the Bank of India, Arthur Eddington, Britain's famous physicist, and many others well known in the 20th century were mystics. Virtually every country in the world has had, and now has, mystics.

Studies say that infants, and many young children, have a partial universal consciousness until their ego and individuality are fully formed. Do we learn how *not* to be mystics? A few do contend that *some* persons who have mental abnormalities may be better able to realize oneness because they do not cling to concepts which block unitary experiences. Humans must transcend self-consciousness; other beings need not ... do some of them view life like mystics?

Religions, sciences and the vast majority of people usually focus on this life on Earth. In perspective, our planet is only a tiny portion of the known Universe, which itself remains mostly unknown to us. The divine essence both pervades and transcends this Universe.

Note: World population grew from 3 billion in 1960 to 7 billion in 2011, more than doubling in 50 years.

Duel of the Dual

"CONSCIENCE" IS A MISUSED and misunderstood word. "Have you no conscience?," ask people of a person who does something which seems to them to be so obviously wrong. Each person has a dual conscience and, occasionally, these two sides do engage in a *duel*.

The Penguin Dictionary of Psychology defines conscience as "*a reasonably coherent set of internalized moral principals that provides evaluations of right and wrong with regard to acts either performed or contemplated. Historically, theistic views aligned conscience with the voice of God and hence regarded it as innate. The contemporary view is that the prohibitions and obligations of conscience are learned ...* " Individual moral development is based on both. Morality applies to personal conduct; ethical to idealized standards.

The Dictionary of Philosophy and Religion lists some interesting historical observations on the word. Socrates said that conscience was the inner warning voice of God. Among Stoics it was a divine spark in man. Throughout the Middle Ages, conscience, *synderesis* in Greek, was universally binding rules of conduct. Religious interpretations later changed in psychiatry.

Sigmund Freud had coined a new term for conscience; he called it "superego." This was self-imposed standards of behavior we learned from parents and our community, rather than from a divine source. People who transgressed those rules felt guilt. Carl Jung, Freud's famous contemporary, said that conscience was an archetype of a "collective unconscious"; content from society is learned later. Most religions still view conscience as the foundation of morality.

Sri Aurobindo said "... true original Conscience in us [is] deeper than constructed and conventional conscience of the moralist, for it is this which points always towards Truth and Right and Beauty, towards Love and Harmony and all that is a divine possibility in us." Perhaps conscience can be viewed as a double-pane window, with the self in between. On one side, it looks toward ego and free will to obey community's laws. On the other side, it is toward the soul and divine will to follow universal law. They often converge to dictate the same, or a similar, course of conduct ... and sometimes not.

The moral dilemma is when these two views conflict. Disobey the laws of society and you might be ostracized and/or go to prison. Disobeying divine law is a sin in most Western religions and causes bad karma, negative consequences, in Eastern faiths. Divine law, or *dharma* in Sanskrit—*logos* in Greek—is fundamental within both Hinduism and Buddhism. It has many definitions and applications.*

"Hinduism" was first used by British scholars for the religions of the people of the Indus valley. Many people

---

* Dharma, or logos, can also mean the source of world order, cosmic reason, moral teachings, individual duty, etc. Unlike dharma, logos more commonly refers to human reason, e.g. logic. In Christianity, Logos is God's Word (wisdom) incarnate in Jesus.

in India refer to their faith as *sanatana dharma*, the absolute and eternal law. Siddharta Gautama, called the Buddha for Awakened or Enlightened Being, founded "Buddhism," correctly named *Buddhadharma*, Buddha's teaching of the eternal Truth, or *Buddhasasana*, practice of those teachings. Universal law supersedes all worldly laws.

Science only considers *natural* law, which it then tries to codify in theories or principles. A sign may ask you to "keep off the grass," but while on it the law of gravity keeps you there. Although society tells you to reset the time, standard vs. daylight saving, you cannot change the 24-hour rotation of Earth. Natural law is divine law as manifest here and now. You can never escape from it in this life.

The laws of our community, or religion, should be followed only when they do not conflict with divine law. Intuitive, innate and interior conscience tells us, without words, what divine will dictates. Reasoned, learned and exterior conscience tells us, with words, what society or religion expects, or demands, of us. Mystics listen to the divine silent voice. It requires listening beyond the self.

Divine conscience is "knowing in your heart" rather than in your mind. In these essays it does occur three times. "It motivates you to respond to the divine will which the soul, through your conscience, tells you is right." It is that critical observer of our self: innate with respect to the divine, not the superego related to our community. "Surface soul is a self's reflection in the divine; conscience opens the soul's depths to reflect the divine essence in this self's life."

Follow your conscience: you will seldom go wrong. The window of your ego is usually clear, although what your parents had taught as "right" may differ from what others claim. The window to the soul may be opaque, but that *inner voice* should be listened to. Intuitive actions might be innate; reasoned conduct is usually learned. The duel must be fought. Too many people try to avoid that encounter.

> Note: The term "Hindu" was used earlier by Arabs, Greeks and Persians for the people of India, which they called "Hindustan."

Asleep

WE ARE ASLEEP about sleep. It occupies almost one-third of most people's lives, which is the reason this essay was written. For that consideration alone, sleep cannot be ignored. Unfortunately, it also involves speculation, imaginings, and some questionable theories and beliefs. As a part of the mystical quest, sleep must be evaluated with great caution. You cannot live always in it nor live without it.

Sleep is usually studied from one of three aspects: its necessity for human life, the meanings of dreams or the state of dreamless sleep. Everyone acknowledges that sleep is essential: it helps to quiet the emotions which might otherwise cause harm; it allows the mind to cleanse itself so that it can function more clearly; the physical body requires rest so that it can "recharge" itself. These descriptions can vary between psychology and physiology, but the need is recognized by all. Many people are "sleep deprived"; a few sleep too much.

Dreams are probably the most controversial aspect of sleep. Some psychiatrists have used dream interpretation to help to reveal repressed thoughts and emotions of the unconscious mind. Some religious persons, including a few mystics, have described *visions* of saints, prophets, angels, or other celestial beings, some of whom *spoke* to them during their dreaming. Many other people believe that dreams are frequently caused by short-term mental and/or physical factors, usually independent of our repressed thoughts and emotions, or any spiritual input. They are a tool, though never real.

The most important aspect of sleep, especially in mysticism, is the dreamless state. Many psychologists and physiologists believe that deep, dreamless sleep is vital for complete rest and rejuvenation of the mind and body. Those people who seem to dream incessantly might often wake up more tired than when they went to bed. Many mystics do claim a parallel between deep meditation and dreamless sleep. In both cases, ego and individuality are forgotten, the sense of self and other are absent, and pure consciousness is actuated.

Few mystics equate dreamless sleep with divine union, yet few would rule it out entirely. Given their assumption divine essence is within every person, but because it is usually unrealized, dreamless sleep might be necessary for us to reunite with our true self, with the source and spirit of our being. Not all mystics would agree and most psychiatrists, physiologists and non-religious persons would not even consider it. It is, however, temporary and not conscious.

Mystical experiences are often described as *consciousness* of the unity of existence, of universal oneness, or union with the divine. Is sleep, in either dreams or dreamless, conscious? Most would say it is semi-conscious. An unconscious person would seldom be revived by an alarm clock, turning on lights or bright sunshine. Of course, a few people can sleep through each. Some persons say that they are "conscious" of their dreams. Fortunately, we forget most of them; we could confuse them with the experiences in our waking state.

Activity of dreaming can be measured, even though we cannot "see into" dreams of others. Recorded by an EEG, PET, SPECT, or fMRI, there seems to be a direct correlation in brain wave activity during states of dreamless sleep and deep meditation vis-à-vis those of dreaming and a relaxed waking state. The content of the former cannot be compared because they cannot be determined. Scarcely anyone remembers intervals of dreamless sleep; they just wake up more refreshed. Few people who meditate can describe a period of *samadhi*. The parallels are not exact, although quite similar.

What happened at home or work? What did you drink or eat late at night? What did you watch, read or listen to just before bedtime? Worried about tomorrow? One or more of those factors might have affected your dreams. What about dreamless sleep? Perhaps it was facilitated by a satisfying day, resolving a problem, meditation, or prayer. Sleep is still quite a mystery, even if some have measured it and others have interpreted it. We need it, yet don't fully understand it.

Many perpetual mystics require little sleep; two or three hours in the dreamless state is often enough for them. Unfortunately, some people suffer from insomnia; lying in bed does not assure sufficient sleep. Most move gradually from a waking state to drowsiness, then alternately, to dreamless sleep and dreams. Meditators may move from a normal waking to a deeper awakening; some do get drowsy. Accomplished mystics seem able to nap in deep sleep, or go in and out of samadhi, while in brief periods of inactivity during the day.

Most dreams are a onetime occurrence. Repetitive dreams can have more significance. Sleep could be an escape. Psychotherapists will want to know "from what?" Sleep might be a release. Spiritual teachers want to know "toward what?" Wake up about sleep! We need rest, but can be asleep about Reality for the rest of our lives.

> Note: Hinduism tells of a fourth, "turiya," beyond waking, dreaming and deep sleep. It is direct awareness of divine oneness in absolute consciousness … constantly actuated by saints during this life. It is the greatest achievement of great lives.

Be Realistic

MYSTICAL EXPERIENCES WILL not resolve all your emotional, mental and physical problems. While seeking, those personal concerns may block or, at least, slow your progress on the path. It *will* only while absorbed in them. What happens afterwards depends upon you.

Mysticism is not about *you*. It is about the ground of existence, the very nature of being itself. If you are just concerned with your own achievement, with escaping your troubles and judge advancement solely in relation to yourself, true divine awareness will elude you. While you cannot transcend your surface self, you cannot reach the absolute and ultimate. You will remain entwined in the temporary and relative. You create your own limitations, even if you prefer not to acknowledge it. "You" is insignificant; *beyond you* is essential.

Whenever students arrive at school burdened with their personal worries, selfish interests and multiple hang-ups, they cannot learn. They may hear what is being said, but will not understand it because they are not paying attention or are filtering it through their ego. What *is*, not what you want it to be.

Most of these essays have a similar message: Forget about your *self*. The affective "I" of ego, psychological "me" of individuality, and material "my" of your manifest being must be absent to experience divine Reality. Why crave love, or lament past loves, when divine Love surrounds you? How can you find divine Truth while occupied with everyday fictions and fantasies? You want what you want when you want it ... yet are seldom able to specify exactly what you want. What we most long for, *wholeness*, is beyond our ability to explain.

When we study what we emotionally feel, mentally conceive or physically perceive in this life, we begin to realize that much of it is based on our own assumptions rather than demonstrable facts. We rarely can, by ourselves, truly prove most of what we believe has already been proven to be true. As Oscar Wilde once said, "when you *'assume'* you make an ass out of you and me." What we each imagine to be correct is frequently confused with fact. It is not that people are stupid or naive, it is just that we are "too busy" (too lazy?) to confirm our beliefs. Ignorance is *not* bliss ... it breeds lethargy.

Knowing what *is* in this life may be limited by our expectations, our defenses and lack of attention. What we presuppose to be true, protecting ourselves in case it is not, and preoccupation with other matters, cloud our perceptions. We may feel someone loves us, yet think they possibly are using us, or saying and doing what will trap us. Unconditional love cannot be realized on those terms. The best things in life[**] must be accepted for what they are, even at the risk they are not. Absorption in divine essence, mystical union, is such.

[**] The best things in life—this life or the eternal—are not free. They require dedication.

"What if such an encounter is misinterpreted, just a fiction of our imagination or is a sign of insanity?" If we think any of those things, we will probably end that experience. In so doing, we may have blocked the flow of divine Love, Truth and Reality. Isn't the risk worth that reward? You bought a lottery ticket knowing that your chances of winning were minuscule. How about spending a little of your immediate *self* to reach the eternal? "Someone has to win."

"What if it is not mystical consciousness?" Then you only lost a few moments of your life. We often waste hours or days in activities which got us nowhere. Have you ever thought about opportunities you had missed because you were unwilling to take a chance? Some may have led to nothing; others could have brought great happiness or other benefits. Most of our life has some risk. Crossing the street is more dangerous than most projected or imagined threats.

We frequently choose to keep what we have and know—even if we concede that it might not be very much—rather than gamble on getting something unknown, although it could be greater than anything which we have ever had. Some people are "afraid of their own shadow." Actually, most of us are frightened of too much light. When carefully examining our assumptions, especially those we have long accepted to be true, we might find that some were based on inaccurate or incomplete information. That requires a shift in belief; some may call it a paradigm shift. It can be uncomfortable.

You might prefer that your established beliefs remain as they are. If so, then give up mysticism. Mystics had to revise their personal beliefs often during the quest. Mystical absorptions, *as steps toward enlightenment*, are usually momentary or, only rarely, for hours. The greatest achievement in life is when those experiences transform your being. They may be brief flashes of insight which highlight a spiritual life, but are a constant source of energy for divine living.

Being realistic requires facing the truth. Being in the Real is to *know* the True. It is the greatest degree of existence here and now.

Mystics' Consciousness

THE ESSENCE OF MYSTICS' consciousness is suprarational, beyond reason, logic or images. It cannot beexplained by rational thought, although we keep trying to do so. Mystics unite with eternal Reality which *is*; mysticism speculates on what, how or why it is.

Consciousness in divine oneness, viewed from various historical, cultural and personal perspectives, have occurred with different frequencies, degrees of realization and durations. This can help to explain the diversity in expressions or reports of that spiritual awareness. The ultimate Reality is the same, but absorption in it may differ. That is true for each mystic, as well as between mystics.

Spiritual *knowing*, mystical gnosis, is *complete intuitive insight*. It combines the very definition of all three words. *Complete*: "The entirety needed for realization; consummate." *Intuitive:* "Knowing something without rational processes; the immediate cognition of it." *Insight*: "Discernment of the true nature of a situation; the penetration beyond the reach of the senses." Complete intuitive insight precedes divine unity and usually follows it. Union with the divine, however, transcends knower, known and knowing; it is to be at one with the divine essence.

"It is a condition of consciousness in which feelings are fused, ideas melt into one another, boundaries are broken, and ordinary distinctions transcended. Past and present fade away into a sense of timeless being. Consciousness and being are not different from each other. In this fullness of felt life and freedom, the distinction of the knower and known disappears. The privacy of the individual self is broken into and invaded by a universal self which the individual feels as his own. The experience itself is felt to be sufficient and complete. It does not come in fragmentary or truncated form demanding completion by something else. It does not look beyond itself for meaning or validity."
Sarvepalli Radhakrishnan (H)

"Satori may be defined as an intuitive looking into the nature of things in contradistinction to the analytical or logical understanding of it. Practically, it means the unfolding of a new world heretofore unperceived in the confusion of a dualistically trained mind. ... all its opposites and contradictions are united and harmonized into a consistent organic whole. Satori can thus be had only through our once personally experiencing it." D.T. Suzuki (B)

"It is impossible [to write about it] because all things are interrelated. I can hardly open my mouth to speak without feeling as though the sea burst its dams and overflowed. How then shall I express what my soul has received? How can I set it down in a book?" Isaac Luria (the Ari) (J)

"All that the imagination can imagine and the reason conceive and understand in this life is not, and cannot be, a proximate means of union with God."
St. John of the Cross (C)

"The end of Sufism is total absorption in God ... but in reality that is the beginning of the Sufi life, for those intuitions

and other things which precede it are, so to speak, the porch by which they enter." Abu Hamid Al-Ghazali (I)

"The most beautiful and profound emotion we can experience is the sensation of the mystical. It is the sower of all true science. To know that what is impenetrable to us really exists, manifesting itself as the highest wisdom and most radiant beauty—which our dull faculties can comprehend only in their primitive form—this knowledge, this feeling, is at the center of all religion." Albert Einstein

The ultimate Reality of the divine One—its essence surpassing conception or perception—is absolute certainty for those absorbed in it. It had infused itself into every part of their being, confirming intuitive insight of, and increasing love for, the unity of all existence. Most mystics then returned to their limited human self, many of them greatly transformed, but a few did continue in this universal consciousness for all the remaining years of their mortal life.

A little of that eternal life should be integrated into a little of this life. If our spiritual insights are restricted to periods of meditation or contemplation, they might temporarily enlighten us, but they will not transform us. The perpetual mystics, who some call saints, have been completely transformed in every aspect of their being. They live in the divine every moment. Our learning must be incorporated into our being if we are to progress toward eternal oneness.

Deep meditation can result in the absence of any sense of self and other, which Hindus and Buddhists may call *samadhi*. Most mystics feel eternal union is assured when you give up ego self during this lifetime. Sufis say, "to die before one dies." The Christian mystics call it "death to self." Kabbalists refer to it as *bittul ha-yesh*, "annihilation of the desiring self." Whenever there is no observing "self" then, in transpersonal actuality, there is no "other." In self-less living, all is experienced as unity in essence. The greatest achievement in life is maintaining that realization.

Almost every person feels that their life is lacking in some way, although they are seldom able to define it. There always seems to be *something missing*. True mystics feel *wholeness* often. It is not a temporary absorption in divine union. Rather, it is identifying the divine essence as the ground of being itself. Living, for them, usually expands beyond their own immediate sentiments, thoughts and sensing.

> *"My me is God, nor do I know my selfhood save in Him. My Being is God, not by simple participation, but by true transformation of my Being."* St. Catherine of Genoa (C)

> *"The individual works in the cosmic process no longer as an obscure and limited ego, but as the centre of the divine or universal consciousness embracing and transforming into harmony all individual manifestations. It is to live in the world with one's inward being profoundly modified. Thesoul takes possession of itself and cannot be shaken from its tranquility by the attractions and attacks of the world."* Sarvepalli Radhakrishnan (H)

> *"Your deep soul hides itself from consciousness. So you need to increase ... elevation of thinking, penetration of thought, liberation of mind—until finally your soul reveals itself to you. Then you find bliss ... by attaining equanimity, by becoming one with everything that happens, by reducing yourself so extremely that you nullify your individual, imaginary form."* Abraham Isaac Kook (J)

"... the annihilation of the ego-conception, freedom from subjectivity, insight into the essence of Suchness, the recognition of the oneness of existence." Ashvaghosha (B)

"He who knows Reality, to whom Unicity is revealed, sees at first gaze the Light of Being. He perceives by illumination that pure light. He sees God first in everything he sees." Mahmoud Shabestari (I)

Whether mystical experiences vary in their cultural context, or are similar for all true mystics, is less important than that they transform each one's sense of being to a transpersonal outlook on all life. Mystics' worldview surpass individual differences. Their higher regard is for the commonality, community and communion amongst all.

Specialized Bibliography

Books on special aspects of mysticism are listed (✳ multiple applications). Titles in bold print are not in the primary bibliography. Those included on the sciences do not prove mysticism; most, however, do support it.

Psychology and Psychiatry

Psychoanalysis and Buddhism: An Unfolding Dialogue
  Edited by Jeremy D. Safran. Published by Wisdom Publications 2003

Toward a Psychology of Awakening
  John Welwood, Ph.D.. Published by Shambhala 2000, 2002

Yoga & Psychotherapy: Evolution of Consciousness
  Rama, Ballentine, Ajaya. Published by Himalayan International Institute 1978, 1981

Sacred Therapy: Jewish Spiritual Teachings
  Estelle Frankel. Published by Shambhala 2003

Exploring Mysticism: A Methodological Essay
  Frits Staal. Published by University of California Press 1975

Living Deeply: The Art and Science of Transformation in Everyday Life
  M. Schiltz, C. Vieten, T. Amorok. Published by New Harbinger Publications 2007

Mysticism, Mind, Consciousness
  Robert K.C. Forman. Published by State University of New York Press 1999 *

One Cosmos under God: The Unification of Matter, Life, Mind and Spirit
  Robert W. Godwin. Published by Paragon House 2004 *

Transcending the Levels of Consciousness
  David R. Hawkins, M.D., Ph.D.. Published by Veritas Publishing 2006

Dictionary of Psychology
  Edited by Arthur S. Reber & Emily S. Reber. Published by Penguin Books 1985, 2001 *

Biology and Neurology

Zen and the Brain: Toward an Understanding of Meditation and Consciousness
  James H. Austin, M.D.. Published by MIT Press 1998, 1999

The God Gene: How Faith is Hardwired into Our Genes
  Dean Hamer, Ph.D.. Published by Anchor Books/Random House 2004

The Mystical Mind: Probing the Biology of Religious Experience
  Newberg & D'Aquili. Published by Fortress Press 1999

Mysticism, Mind, Consciousness
  Robert K.C. Forman. Published by State University of New York Press 1999 *

One Cosmos under God: The Unification of Matter, Life,

Mind and Spirit
  Robert W. Godwin. Published by Paragon House 2004 *

The Spiritual Brain: A Neuroscientist's Case for the Existence of the Soul
  M. Beauregard, D. O'Leary. Published by HarperCollins 2007

Spiritual Evolution: Scientists Discuss Their Beliefs
  Edited by John Marks Templeton. Published by Templeton Foundation Press 1998 *

Why God Won't Go Away: Brain Science and the Biology of Belief
  A. Newberg, E. D'Aquili. Published by Ballantine 2001

Dictionary of Psychology
  Edited by Arthur S. Reber & Emily S. Reber. Published by Penguin Books 1985, 2001 *

Physics and Astronomy

The God Theory: Universes, Zero-point Fields
  What's Behind It All, by Bernard Haisch, Ph.D.. Published by Weiser Books 2006

One Cosmos under God: The Unification of Matter, Life, Mind and Spirit
  Robert W. Godwin. Published by Paragon House 2004 *

Quantum Questions: Mystical Writings of the World's Great Physicists
  Edited by Ken Wilber. Published by Shambhala 1984, 2001

Quantum Theology: Spiritual Implications of the New Physics
   Diarmuid O'Murchu. Published by Crossroad Publishing 2004

Spiritual Evolution: Scientists Discuss Their Beliefs
   Edited by John Marks Templeton. Published by Templeton Foundation Press 1998 *

The Spiritual Universe: One Physicist's Vision of Spirit, Soul, Matter, and Self
   Fred Alan Wolf. Published by Moment Point Press 1996, 1999

The Visionary Window: A Quantum Physicist's Guide to Enlightenment
   A. Goswami. Published by Quest Books 2000, 2006

God in the Equation: How Einstein Transformed Religion
   Corey S. Powell. Published by Free Press / Simon and Schuster 2002, 2005

Female Mystics

Women's Buddhism: Buddhism's Women
   Edited by Ellison Banks Findly. Published by Wisdom Publications 2000

The Experience of No-Self: A Contemplative Journey
   Bernadette Roberts. Published by Shambhala 1982, 1993

The Flowering of Mysticism: Men and Women in the New Mysticism: 1200-1350
   Bernard McGinn. Published by Crossroad Publishing 1998

Mystics of the Christian Tradition
   Steven Fanning. Published by Routledge 2001

Daughters of the Goddess: Women Saints of India
   Linda Johnsen. Published by Yes International 1994

Women of Sufism: A Hidden Treasure
   Selected by Camille Adams Helminski. Published by Shambhala 2003

Mysticism: A Study in Nature and Development of Spiritual Consciousness
   Evelyn Underhill. Published currently by KDP 1911, 2011

The Receiving: Reclaiming Jewish Women's Wisdom
   Rabbi Tirzah Firestone. Published by Harper San Francisco 2002

The Spiral Path: Explorations into Women's Spirituality
   Edited by Theresa King. Published by Yes International 1992

Surprised by Grace: A Journey Beyond Personal Enlightenment
   Amber Terrell. Published by True Light Publishing 1997

Orthodox (Institutional) Religion

Three Ways of Asian Wisdom
   Nancy Wilson Ross. Published by Simon and Schuster 1966, 1996 H/B

The Concise Guide to World Religions
   Eliade and Couliano. Published by HarperCollins San Francisco 1991, 2000

God: A Brief History: The Human Search for Eternal Truth
John Bowker. Published by DK Publishing 2002

A History of God: The 4, 000-Year Quest of Judaism, Christianity and Islam
Karen Armstrong. Published by Gramercy Books 1993, 2004

The New Penguin Handbook of Living Religions
Edited by John R. Hinnells. Published by Penguin Books 1997, 2003

Oxford Dictionary of World Religions
Edited by John Bowker. Published by Oxford University Press 1997, 2005 *

The Religion Book: Encyclopedia of Places, Prophets, Saints, & Seers
J. Willis. Published by Visible Ink 2004

World Religions: From Ancient History to the Present
Edited by Geoffrey Parriner. Published by Facts on File Inc. 1971, 1985

Death and Afterlife

The Tibetan Book of the Dead
W.Y. Evans-Wentz & Kazi Dawa-Samdup. Published by Oxford University Press 1927, 2005

Graceful Exists: How Great Beings Die
Edited by Sushila Blackman. Published by Shambhala 1997, 2005

Life after Death in World Religions
Edited by Harold Coward. Published by Orbis Books 1997

SPECIALIZED BIBLIOGRAPHY 215

Oxford Dictionary of World Religions
Edited by John Bowker. Published by Oxford University Press 1997, 2000 *

> Note: None of these essays quoted sacred scriptures (although many books in the bibliography do); there could be no end to that technique. Two texts were quoted. The Zohar in Judaism is the primary mystical text of Kabbalah, yet not contained in the Torah or in any of the Hebrew Bible. The Bhagavad-gita in Hinduism is a revered part of an epic poem, but is not in the ancient Vedas or the later Upanishads. Revelation is not limited to holy books. What is experienced is more important than what is read.

[These essays have omitted diacritical marks. Some non-phonetic pronunciations: Gnosis is nosis; Jnana is gyana; Panna is pannya; Prajna is prajnya]

Secondary Bibliography

There are thousands of books on mysticism so it can be difficult to decide which to buy. The following were read, but then were omitted for various reasons. The 100 books in the primary bibliography were more useful than these publications. Your recommendations of other sources are welcome.

Buddhism *(omitted)*

A Concise History of Buddhism
 Andrew Skilton

Early Madhyamika in India and China
 Richard H. Robinson

The Tibetan Book of the Dead
 W.Y. Evans-Wentz & Lama Dawa-Samdup

What the Buddha Taught
 Rev. Walpola Rahula

Women of the Way: Discovering 2,500 Years of Buddhist Wisdom
 Edited by Sallie Tisdale

Christianity *(omitted)*

The Courage to Be
 Paul Tillich

The Heart of Matter
   Pierre Teilhard de Chardin

The Journal of George Fox
   Edited by Rufus M. Jones

Meister Eckhart: Selected Writings
   Translated by O. Davies

St. John of the Cross
   Translated with commentary by Antonio T. de Nicolas

Hinduism *(omitted)*

Autobiography of a Yogi
   A.C. Pramahansa Yogananda

Essays on the Gita (aka Bhagavad-gita and its message)
   Sri Aurobindo

Hinduism
   Louis Renou

How to Know God: Yoga Aphorisms of Patanjali
   Prabhavananda & Isherwood

The Life and Teachings of Sai Baba of Shirdi
   Antonio Rigopoulos

Samadhi Yoga
   Swami Sivananda

A Source Book of Modern Hinduism
   Edited by Glyn Richards

Who Cares?!: The Unique Teaching of Ramesh S. Balsekar
   Edited by Blayne Bardo

Islam *(omitted)*

The Inner Life
  Hazrat Inayat Khan

The Other Islam: Sufism and the road to global harmony
  Stephen Schwartz

Knowledge of God in Classical Sufism
  Translated and intro. by John Renard

Steps to Freedom / Discourses on the Alchemy of the Heart
  Reshad Feild

Sufi Studies: East and West
  Edited by L.F. Rushbrook Williams

Sufi Thought and Action
  Assembled by Idries Shah

The Sufis
  Idries Shah

Sufism, Veil and Quintessence
  Frithjof Schuon

Judaism *(omitted)*

Abraham Isaac Kook
  Translation & introduction by Ben Zion Bokser

The Jewish Lights Spirituality Handbook
  Edited by Stuart M. Matlins

Let There be Light: Modern Cosmology and Kabblah
  Howard A. Smith

9 1/2 Mystics: The Kabbalah Today
  Herbert Weiner

On the Kabbalah and its Symbolism
  Gershom Scholem

The Receiving: Reclaiming Jewish Women's Wisdom
  Rabbi Tirzah Firestone

Comparative Studies *(omitted)*

Coming Home: Experience of Enlightenment in Sacred Traditons
  Lex Hixon

Tantra: The Path of Ecstasy
  Georg Feuerstein

Wisdom of the Sadhu: Teachings of Sundar Singh
  Edited by Kim Comer

Mysticism *(omitted)*

The Complete Guide to World Mysticism
  Timothy Freke and Peter Gandy

Cosmic Consciousness
  Richard Maurice Bucke, M.D.

Escape Your Own Prison: Why We Need Spirituality and Psychology to be Truly Free
  Bernard Starr, Ph.D.

Essential Spirituality: The 7 Central Practices to Awaken Heart and Mind
  Roger Walsh, M.D., Ph.D.

SECONDARY BIBLIOGRAPHY

Exploring Mysticism: A Methodological Essay
  Frits Staal

The God Theory: Universes, Zero-Point Fields, and What's Behind It All
  Bernard Haisch, Ph.D.

The Holy Longing: Hidden Power of Spiritual Yearning
  Connie Zweig

Holy Madness: Spirituality, Crazy-Wise Teachers, and Enlightenment
  Georg Feuerstein

The Human Cycle
  Sri Aurobindo

Inner Journey Home: The Soul's Realization of the Unity of Reality
  A.H. Almaas

Measuring the Immeasurable: Scientific Case for Spirituality
  Numerous authors

Mystical Consciousness: Western Perspectives and Dialogue with Japanese Thinkers
  Louis Roy, O.P.

A New Earth: Awakening to Your Life's Purpose
  Eckhart Tolle

Phenomenology of Spirit
  G.W.F. Hegel

Rational Mysticism: Spirituality Meets Science in the Search For Enlightenment
  John Horgan

The Spiral Path: Explorations into Women's Spirituality
  Edited by Theresa King

Spiritual Genius: 10 Masters and the Quest for Meaning
  Winifred Gallagher

The Spiritual Universe: One Physicist's Vision of Spirit, Soul, Matter, and Self
  Fred Alan Wolf

Transformations in Consciousness,
  Franklin Merrell-Wolff

The Varieties of Religious Experience
  William James

Western Spirituality: Historical Roots, Ecumenical Routes
  Edited by Matthew Fox

Other References *(omitted)*

The Paperback of the The Biology of Transcendence: A Blueprint of the Human Spirit
  Joseph Chilton Pearce

Black Holes and Baby Universes
  Stephen Hawking

A Concise Dictionary of Indian Philosophy
  Edited by John Grimes

Cosmic Jackpot: Why Our Universe is Just Right for Life
  Paul Davies

Dark Cosmos: In Search of Our Universe's Missing Mass and Energy
  Dan Hooper

SECONDARY BIBLIOGRAPHY

Encyclopedia of the World's Religions
 Edited by R.C. Zaehner

Endless Universe: Beyond the Big Bang
 Paul J. Steinhardt & Neil Turok

The Fabric of the Cosmos
 Brian Greene

The God Gene: How Faith is Hardwired into Our Genes
 Dean Hamer, Ph.D.

The God Particle: If the Universe Is the Answer, What Is the Question?
 Leon Lederman & Dick Teresi

God's Equation: Einstein, Relativity, and the Expanding Universe
 Amir Aczel

A History of Religious Ideas: Volume 3
 Mircea Eliade

How to Know God: Soul's Journey into Mystery of Mysteries
 Deepak Chopra

The Ideal of Human Unity
 Sri Aurobindo

Integral Consciousness and the Future of Evolution
 Steve McIntosh

Intelligence in Nature: An Inquiry into Knowledge
 Jeremy Narby

Jung on Evil
 Edited by Murray Stein

The Language of God
  Francis S. Collins (head-Human Genome Project)

Microcosmos: Discovering the World Through Microscopic Images
  Brandon Broll

Mind, Life, and Universe
  Edited by Lynn Margulis and Eduardo Punset

My Stroke of Insight: A Brain Scientist's Personal Journey
  Jill Bolte Taylor

Science and the Reenchantment of the Cosmos: The Rise of the Integral Vision of Reality
  Ervin Lazlo

Universe: A Journey from Earth to the Edge of the Cosmos
  Nicolas Cheetham

Wholeness and the Implicate Order
  David Bohm

www.ingramcontent.com/pod-product-compliance
Lightning Source LLC
Chambersburg PA
CBHW051427290426
44109CB00016B/1462